Peeling Potatoes, Painting Pictures

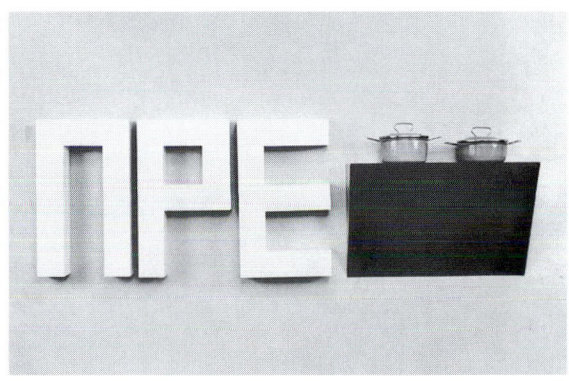

The Dodge Soviet Nonconformist Art Publication Series

Copublished by the Jane Voorhees Zimmerli Art Museum and Rutgers University Press

The Norton and Nancy Dodge Collection of nearly twenty thousand works of Nonconformist Art from the Soviet Union, 1956–1986, is part of the Jane Voorhees Zimmerli Art Museum at Rutgers University, New Brunswick, New Jersey.

Peeling Potatoes, Painting Pictures

Women Artists in Post-Soviet Russia, Estonia, and Latvia
THE FIRST DECADE

Renee Baigell
and Matthew Baigell

A COPUBLICATION OF
THE JANE VOORHEES ZIMMERLI ART MUSEUM
AND RUTGERS UNIVERSITY PRESS
NEW BRUNSWICK, NEW JERSEY, AND LONDON

Library of Congress Cataloging-in-Publication Data

Baigell, Renee.
    Peeling potatoes, painting pictures : women artists in post-Soviet Russia, Estonia, and Latvia :
the first decade / Renee Baigell and Matthew Baigell.
      p. cm.
    Includes bibliographical references and index.
    ISBN 0-8135-2945-X (cloth : alk. paper) — ISBN 0-8135-2946-8 (pbk. : alk paper)
      1. Feminism and art—Russia (Federation)   2. Women artists—Russia (Federation)—
Interviews.   3. Feminism and art—Estonia.   4. Women artists—Estonia—Interviews.
5. Feminism and art—Latvia.   6. Women artists—Latvia—Interviews.   I. Baigell, Matthew.
II. Title.
N72.F45 B345 2001
704′.042′094709049—dc21   00-046872

British Cataloging-in-Publication data for this book is available from the British Library.

Manufactured in the United States of America

FOR LEAH AND NAOMI

Contents

Illustrations

Preface

THIS BOOK grew naturally and inevitably from our previous joint effort, *Soviet Dissident Art: Interviews after Perestroika,* which the Rutgers University Press published in 1995. For that book, we asked artists about their lives as dissident or underground artists in the late Soviet era. During a number of interviews with women, it became apparent that other kinds of stories needed to be told, one of which concerns issues and problems they faced as women living in an insistently patriarchal society. For some, it seemed to make no difference if they were discussing aspects of their lives in the pre- or post-Soviet period. Nothing or very little had changed for them as women. For others, there was some sense of hope and even change. This story constitutes the present book.

As before, Renee conducted the interviews in Russian. Matthew held the tape recorder. Altogether, we visited the homes and studios of eighty-five artists in Moscow, St. Petersburg, Talinn, Riga, and New York between 1995 and 2000. Names were initially provided by Norton Dodge, whose collection, the Norton and Nancy Dodge Collection of Nonconformist Art from the Soviet Union, is housed in the Zimmerli Art Museum at Rutgers; and by Alla Rosenfeld, curator of the Russian and Soviet Collections. In each of the foreign cities we visited, the artists were gracious enough to introduce us to friends and colleagues and, in effect, to pass us around. Some whom we wanted to interview, were out of town unavailable, or refused to speak with us. Although there is obviously a randomness factor, we feel that we saw a representative group of artists. The oldest were born in the 1920s and 1930s. Most were born during and after World War II, several in the 1960s, and two in the 1970s. Many had been married to and divorced from artists. Some had remarried artists. Others preferred their independence. Many had at least one child. We interviewed such important artists as Dzemma

Skulme, the president of the Latvian artists' union; Viva Tole, considered to be the dean of Estonian graphic artists; Natalia Nestevera and Tatiana Nazarenko, two Moscow-based artists who, although we could never get precise answers about this, were persons of some power in the art unions during the Soviet period; Aidan Salakhova and other gallery owners; Natalia Kamenetskaia, probably the major feminist in the Russian art world; a few art critics; and a variety of painters, sculptors, graphic artists, collagists, photographers, and installation and performance artists whose styles range from conservative to cutting edge and whose attitudes toward women's issues range from hostile to deeply committed.

Because of the patriarchal nature of east European society, some women and all of the men (some husbands insisted on being present at the interviews) initially looked at Matthew when answering Renee's questions. Early on, he had decided not to respond to body language or to smiles, but rather to sit stony-faced so that the interviewees would have to interact directly with Renee. We mention this here because it indicates a certain kind of mindset we encountered, one that unfortunately helped set the tone of the responses of several women to Renee's questions.

In addition to Norton Dodge, Alla Rosenfeld, and Dennis Cate, we want to thank Dr. Natalia Barbash, who transcribed the tapes, which were then translated into English by Renee. We also want to thank Tod Weinberg of New Europe, LTD, and his staff in Moscow and St. Petersburg for facilitating the interviews in those cities. Leslie Mitchner, editor in chief at Rutgers University Press, was, as always, her wonderfully encouraging self. Thanks also to our copyeditor, Romaine Perin, and production coordinator Tricia Politi.

Peeling Potatoes, Painting Pictures

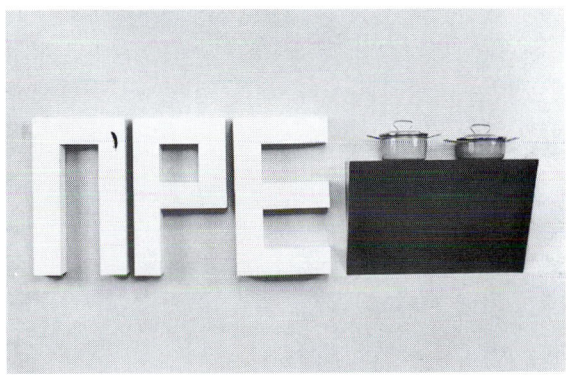

Introduction

WE WANT to explain the title at the outset. During our interview with the Latvian artist Malda Muizule, she said that she is the family breadwinner and that her husband believes that she has a gift from God, in her being able to switch quickly from peeling potatoes to painting pictures. Although we also interviewed sculptors, photographers, performance artists, critics, and gallery owners who do not paint pictures, we discovered that Muizule's husband's observation, at least the part about potatoes and painting, had the ring of truth, one that will become increasingly evident through the pages of this book.

When we interviewed Lydia Masterkova a few years ago for our book on Soviet dissident artists, she made a comment that was unexpected and out of context.[1] She said, "I bow to no man," and then continued to discuss some aspect of dissident life during the Soviet era. Here was one of the few heroines of the dissident movement, one of the group of artists who lived in Lionozovo, a town outside Moscow, interjecting into the conversation a statement that may have had more profound meaning for her than her answers to our questions about nonconformist life during the Brezhnev era. She was one of the first dissident artists, an expatriate by 1976, having been basically kicked out of her country, now living a quiet life in a small French town near the Luxembourg border, but in the stir of memories our questions must have provoked, the male-female issue rose to the forefront of her consciousness. Despite repeated questions on our part, she had nothing further to say about the matter. All this was provocative, to say the least, and it indicated to us that although she denied the presence of a problem, she also inadvertently admitted that there was one.

We soon realized that she had no framework with which to discuss her seemingly offhanded comment, and no language with which to consider women's issues, let alone anything remotely connected with a feminist point of view. These matters, central to the lives of so many Western artists for years, were simply invisible to her. They did not exist. Whatever had been the actual facts of her life, the experiences she had had as a woman living in the Soviet Union, she believed—as she had been taught—that men and women were equal. She revealed absolutely no interest in any kind of special pleading (affirmative action) because this would have been tantamount to admitting that men were better artists. To argue in this way, she held, would in effect conflate issues concerning the quality of her art with her position as a woman in Soviet society. These were two separate things. Art was art, and society was something else. We knew that there was material here for further exploration after the book on dissident artists was completed.

A subsequent search through the literature on women's issues during the Soviet and post-Soviet years indicated that a considerable amount of material had been published, but shockingly little on such concerns in the art world—a few articles but no extensive study of the issues women artists faced as women.[2] We thought that data collected from a reasonable number of interviews would let us know more specifically why somebody such as Masterkova had no framework or language with which to discuss such matters, and how others managed their private and professional lives in what was and still is a profoundly patriarchic society. We realized that this would be the first book-length assessment of how women artists in the post-Soviet period viewed themselves as women artists, what they thought of feminism in general, and what, if any, changes took place during the decade of the 1990s. And, because several of the artists we hoped to interview had gone to school during the Soviet era, we would also learn something about their lives as artists during that earlier period. It was our hope in undertaking this project that we might provide firsthand information about these women, call attention to their situation, and contribute to the general history of Russian (and east European) art in the immediate post-Soviet era, to offer something equivalent to the many studies available in the fields of literature, political science, and sociology.[3]

There is not a lot of history on which to ground this study. A summary account would begin around the end of the nineteenth century when, in response to the growing interest in the development of a Russian national art, women were encouraged to make handicrafts based on folk art sources, a creative outlet thought to be appropriate for them. Figures such as Elena Polanova (1850–1898), Princess Maria Tenisheva, and Maria Yakunchikova (1870–1902) organized arts and crafts schools in pursuit of this goal.[4] But such efforts, however well intentioned, relegated women to second-tier status by confirming the general opinion that they could not and should not compete with men in the more serious realm of the fine arts. Evidently, this is still a strongly held opinion. Given the patriarchal nature of Russian society, we were not surprised when several contemporary artists told us that many men firmly believe that women should not paint or sculpt, but should train for careers in the applied arts or, better yet, stay at home with the children.

We were also not surprised to hear more than once in the 1990s an argument offered more than a century ago concerning the nature of women. For example, Feodor Rerbeg (1865–1938), a founder of the Moscow Association of Artists, insisted that the significance of women artists will grow only when they stop trying to imitate male artists. "They [the women] must stop being ashamed of their own feminine souls and sympathies, and use all of their strength to reveal their beauty of spirit, which is finer and more sensitive that that of men."[5] That is, Rerberg's unstated assumption of biological determinism is still accepted by several contemporary women artists.

Despite these opinions concerning women and the types of art they might create most successfully, women did play an active role in the country's economic life. It is reported that by 1912, women constituted 52 percent of Moscow's labor force and also helped organize workers' strikes when they were called on. However, because of the customary diffidence women exhibited toward men, the former were reluctant to join labor unions, thus allowing the men to lead the fight for better working conditions. Nevertheless, in 1895, women did organize the Russian Mutual Philanthropic Society, which ran day-care centers, and the Women's Progressive Party and the Union for Women's Equality, both in 1905, to ameliorate conditions of working-class women.[6]

Perhaps buoyed by all of these efforts, a generation of powerful women artists emerged in the second decade of the past century committed not to women's issues or to a women's art, but directly to mainstream art and, as a result, became part of the history of modern Russian art. These include Natalia Goncharova (1881–1962), who helped form with Mikhail Larionov the cubist- and fauve-influenced Knave of Diamonds Group in Moscow in 1910 and, a few years later in 1913, signed Larinov's futurist-inspired Rayonnist Manifesto. Nadezhda Udaltsova (1885–1961) worked closely with Malevich and Tatlin and participated in exhibitions in Moscow in the 1910s. Olga Rozanova (1886–1918) wrote her own manifesto, "The Bases of the New Creation and Reasons Why It Is Misunderstood," in 1913.[7] And Lyubov Popova (1889–1924) also exhibited in major modernist shows in the 1910s and was a member of Tatlin's Tower Studio.

The Russian Revolution, of course, changed the normal course of developments for in its immediate aftermath a doctrinal linkage was established between the end of women's oppression on the one hand and the destruction of capitalism and the revocation of private property on the other. The "women's question" had been subsumed by ideological issues. Within a year, the Constitution of 1918 (and those of 1936 and 1977) affirmed equal rights for men and women. But Russian men seemed not to be aware of this affirmation. There was something called equal rights, but something else called equality (*ravenstvo*). The former could be written into law; but the latter, concerning daily activities, behavior patterns, and attitudes toward women, never really did change. The net result was that men worked, tried to rise in the world, and at the end of the day returned home and rested. Women, on the other hand, worked, tried to rise in the world within circumscribed occupations, and after a day's work had to shop, take care of the children, and run the household before they could relax. Men, in effect, had one job; women had two. And so women never did achieve equality. Such organizations as the First All-Russian Congress of Women Workers and Peasants, founded in 1918, and the Department for Work among Women in 1919, were formed to promote support for the new regime, not to take care of women's needs. The subsequent Five-Year Plans emphasized production and economic development to the detriment of women's issues. The new Soviet woman was to be man's equal in the workplace, but also the chief caregiver and homemaker. She was expected to be a happy mother and also a worker for the common welfare. Feminism (or whatever the term then used), problems of physical and psychological abuse, low salaries, discrimination in the job market, concern for medical attention, and the desire for child care became identified with reactionary bourgeois ideology. Feminism and a concern for problems peculiar to women had become discredited.

As a consequence, by the early 1930s women became less visible in the art world. Their voices as women's voices were virtually stilled by the time socialist realism was proclaimed the official art of the land at the First All-Union Conference of Soviet Writers in 1934. Prominent women artists, such as sculptor Vera Mukhina (1889–1963), might emerge, but this occurred rarely and then only in the context of approved socialist realist art. But more important, a break occurred with the past. The works of the women modernists disappeared from view, their example forgotten or reduced to the barest of shadowy memories. There was no past to build on, no tradition to continue. As it did among male artists, the modernist heritage, in whatever form it might take, essentially and quite literally vanished. Furthermore, the art unions created at national (USSR), state (e.g.,

Russia), and local (e.g., Moscow) levels made no provision for women to organize as women nor for platforms through which to air grievances.

Within society as a whole, women suffered from discrimination in virtually all professions. Even if 70 percent of the doctors were women in, say, 1974, their numbers were not reflected in positions of authority and higher administration, areas dominated by men.[8] And despite official concern during the decades of the 1960s and 1970s, little was done to alleviate conditions. Rather, women were constantly exhorted to contribute even greater efforts to economic productivity. For example, no less a figure than Mikhail Gorbachev said in his book *Perestroika* that women should return to their womanly mission of homemaking and child care, yet at the same time achieve more in public life.[9] Women were caught in the double bind of having equal rights but not social equality. Some knew it, and some did not, as one lament by an artist and mother in the 1980s attests. She insisted that she never experienced discrimination as a woman, but did as a mother. Did she suffer as a woman?

> Absolutely not. I've never been discriminated against. No one has ever said that there ought to be a man in my place. No. It's the fact that I'm a mother that gets in the way. Of course employees prefer men because . . . if a child is sick the man keeps working but the wife has to stay home. But it isn't all that bad.

And then she continued by saying that she could recommence her career when the child was about twelve years old.[10]

After the demise of the Soviet system, discrimination still existed and even grew stronger, because of job shortages during the 1990s. During the economic meltdown in 1998, women's concerns were increasingly judged to be frivolous, immoral, and wasteful. Employment was still gender-conditioned, one observer even noting, not surprisingly, that encyclopedias written for children in 1994 still included gender-driven material—hand combat, business opportunities, and machine maintenance for boys and laundry care and cooking for girls.[11]

The symbolic date given for the start of the modern women's movement in Russia is 1979, when Tatiana Mamonova published in what was then Leningrad the samizdat magazine *An Almanac: Women and Russia.*[12] The movement led a largely underground life until the 1990s. When it surfaced, its chief proponents were part of the business rather than cultural world, and only minimally that of the art world. Only one organization seems to have had any connection with the arts—the Moscow Organization of Lesbian Literature and Art, which in the mid-1990s had seven members.[13]

Other organizations were formed, one to sell art by women artists (see Irina Mozhaeva interview), but women artists simply did not respond to feminism in any of its potential manifestations.

The reasons vary, and whatever we had read in the literature concerning the general condemnation of feminism was corroborated in interview after interview. Briefly, many artists, like many men in general, associate the movement with hostility to men, with sexual deviance, with rejection of good manners, with separation of the sexes, with special pleading (suggesting that women are not as good as men artists), with virtually anything but a concern for equality and daily domestic problems. Many still believe, all evidence to the contrary, that equality between the sexes existed in the Soviet Union and exists in the post-Soviet era. Several feel that solving economic problems is far more important than getting involved in a strange and basically imported movement, that to do so would be divisive and, under present conditions, irrelevant. Even those who have some understanding of feminist ideas are distrustful of and even opposed to them. They strike many as products of a divisive special interest that might harm the development of their still newly found freedoms after years of government control and censorship. Feminism requires organization, joining groups, which in the minds of many harks back to Soviet methods of coercion. Will they need membership cards? Must they go to meetings? Further, many women, after working in paid jobs for most of their adult lives, now want to return to their traditional role in the home and become full-time homemakers. That is, they want to be taken care of, to buy consumer goods and luxury items. In this context, the kitchen becomes a "free sphere," a place for a home life free of external impositions. Does feminism mean they must return to the workplace? Does women's liberation mean having to hold down a job? Many were not certain what it meant.

We would add another point that was never discussed in any interview, but that may play a subliminal role in how women artists think about these issues. After the breakup of the Soviet Union, Russia and the former republics, now separate countries, had to reinvent themselves as nations with unique histories. They had to reestablish core narratives to cohere as now separate states, which, for example, in the case of Russia, Chechnya continues to challenge. Feminism or women's issues might therefore be considered centrifugal forces, balkanizing elements, in that they address issues peripheral to stabilizing nationalistic forces (in cultural, not political, terms).

Artists are also at a particular disadvantage, since their work, solitary in nature, inhibits the kinds of networking available to women in the professions. Friendships tend to be personal, and conversations, as we heard repeatedly, were mostly about families and children, not about art. Psychological change seems (or seemed) to be glacial; art historian Alison Hilton reported that when she asked Soviet art historians and artists about feminism in the 1970s and 1980s, "few saw any point to my questions, even in the unofficial art world." [14] This is not meant as a critique, but rather as a reminder that the history of eastern Europe bears no resemblance to that of the West. As one observer noted, "It is not easy to discover and express a personal perspective in a society that has for so long been dominated by slogans." [15]

But it is not just slogans. At the most fundamental level, it is the man-woman thing, and *that*, all agreed, will not change in the foreseeable future. As one artist, Alena Romanova (b. 1949), whose interview is reproduced later, said in a loose combination of irony, resignation, anger, and weariness, but with complete honesty and recognition of her situation:

> It is amusing to hear questions about feminism. We have other problems. Perhaps soon we will have a desire to become feminists, but first one has to know what it means to be a woman. A woman in this country has one role: that is motherhood. In this country, she can only be a mother. And in relationship to men she is also a mother.

All these observations are obviously generalizations. But they hold for several artists who have traveled abroad, even to feminist conferences, and who have been visited and interviewed by Western feminists. It became evident, after a handful of interviews, that even as they communicated in Russian, Renee and some of artists were speaking a different language. Few really had any understanding of feminism as a movement concerned with specific biological needs, domestic arrangements, job discrimination, proper medical attention, and types of subject matter reflecting aspects of their lives; or with gender issues concerning the societal roles assigned to men and women and how these might be culturally constructed. Several artists even resented questions directed to them as women artists. They did not want to be singled out as women. It was that simple. Although all the interviewees were friendly, some were put off, perhaps repelled, by the questions they were asked. We assumed that some had never been asked, let alone asked to conceptualize, such questions. Clearly, there was in our questions an instant challenge to self-identity that caused confusion and provoked some abrupt responses. (A number of husbands who insisted on being present at the interviews grew furious, but that is an issue of male hegemony.) Several women responded to a question by saying, "I had never thought of that before," or "I had never thought of that before in that particular way." Several said that they had found the questions interesting and provocative, and would think about them in the future. What may have started in an interview as a series of questions about the artist's experience as a woman often developed into a discussion of women's issues, what they were and what they were not—mostly what they were not, given the misapprehensions many had about the terms *feminism, feminist,* and *gender issues.*

Like Masterkova years before, several lacked and were not particularly interested in developing a verbal or visual language to express what were clearly bottled-up feelings. They complained about, but rarely questioned, demands on their energies for domestic chores. As art students, they unquestionably accepted the fact that women teachers, common in the lower grades, thinned out considerably in the upper grades. Most agreed that women were more emotional than men, thus implicitly accepting the premise that men created art at a higher level than did women. And they accepted the hard fact that men could exhibit their work more easily. But virtually all took issue with gender endings in the Russian language, as if using the masculine ending for *artist* somehow rectified their situation as women. All preferred to use the masculine word for artist, *khudoznik,* to describe themselves, since with the feminine ending, *khudoznitsa,* it carried pejorative connotations. It implied superficiality, that women painted decoratively or made decorative objects, and, worst of all, that they created "women's pictures," meaning sentimental, sweet pictures vapid in content. By contrast, in the United States many women prefer to be called actors, a gender-free term, rather than actresses, which obviously implies gender, but does not carry the stigma of *khudoznitsa.*

Sorting out the responses was difficult. Conflicting statements were the norm, since different artists had had different experiences in art school, in their careers, and in their travels. Some told us what they thought we wanted to hear or stated how they wanted to present themselves or objected to the Western values we had brought with us. Others changed course in the middle of a conversation because a question triggered an unexpected insight. Contradictions abounded. In several instances, some expressed anger in reaction to their home situation, but at the same time were totally opposed to any kind of feminist activity on their behalf. Some artists were quite articulate, others less so, and major artists provided as much or as little information as minor figures. There was no hierarchy of importance here, especially since, as in the West, there is no cutting-edge style in Russia today.

Is there a story to tell? Yes, definitely. First, we discuss and record in interviews probably for the first time the private lives and situations of contemporary artists, attitudes their parents held in regard to their daughters becoming artists, gender issues in art school, the forging of careers, and domestic concerns. Second, despite their many disclaimers, several artists both implicitly and explicitly have explored a feminist subject matter and do project in their art an awareness of gender differences, and these should be noted. Third, there are women artists who throughout the decade of the 1990s did follow a feminist program and did explore a feminist subject matter within the context of their society. By that we mean that some, among them Natalia Kamenetskaia and Anna Alchuk, knew what they were doing; and others, who were more ambivalent, unwittingly and instinctively accepted and rejected aspects of feminism and feminist subject matter as it suited them. The issues are complex, as are the varied responses, which in many instances can be characterized as ambiguous and even confusing. Fourth, an initial chronology needs to be set down because artists and critics have already forgotten so much.

A chronology is also important because attitudes that emerged in the beginning of the 1990s began to change by the end of the decade. Kamenetskaia, who has been at the center of activity since the late 1980s, recently told us (in 2000) that many Russian women artists are suddenly and finally realizing that they must address those issues that affect their lives as women. A corner has definitely been turned. She says that wrong strategies were used initially that caused hostility and misunderstanding. Early in the 1990s, gender issues were stressed. For most, understanding concepts of patriarchy and fighting male domination were just too overwhelming during perestroika and in the first years of democratic rule. The breathtaking economic, political, and cultural roller coaster rides aside, many also thought that feminism meant their becoming like men—hard, aggressive. Now, Kamenetskaia and others are emphasizing women's issues—day care, better birthing conditions, better marketplace opportunities, self-realization. Of course, gender studies and feminism are intertwined; it is a matter of emphasis, Kamenetskaia says, and she feels that a recognizable feminist movement in art is about to happen. The changes, she says, over the past decade are noticeable and exhilarating, and this is evident in the art as well.

To extract a comprehensible account from the raw data of eighty-five interviews, we have organized the material in the following way. We have mixed together both sociological and art-historical materials. The former includes the consideration of experiences in art school, in forging a career, in domestic matters, and in attitudes toward feminist concerns. The latter includes considerations of particular works of art. The main questions here, of course, lie in what constitutes appropriate subject matter for discussion. Is there a particular female approach to imagery, and is there a female subject matter? To short-circuit these questions, clearly worth several books in their own right, we concentrated on images of the body, since this subject is one that seems to have captured the imagination of many artists, for two principal reasons. First, official Soviet art policy inhibited the making of images of the nude body for its own sake. With democracy, controls were completely lifted and the painting of the nude body became in and of itself an act of freedom. Second, many, without always understanding their motivations, painted images of the body as a statement about their own womanhood whether the particular image was male, female, or androgynous. We do not say "without always understanding their motivations" in a condescending way, but to suggest that with the general suppression of the field of psychology during the Soviet period, understanding motivation and unconscious desires are still largely unknown terrains for many. But no doubt some artists obviously know exactly what they are doing.

The first chapter, "Brief Chronology," includes an overview of a number of art exhibitions mounted during the 1990s, to acquaint the reader with general attitudes toward feminist concerns. "Mature Artists" includes interviews with older artists. Their remarks provide a basic understanding of the problems faced by women in the art world. "The New Generation," the longest chapter, includes interviews with younger artists, critics, and gallery owners who in their remarks reflect the ongoing concerns and changes in attitude that characterize that decade. Both preceding and following each interview, we have added comments appropriate to the interviewee's remarks. We have not included all eighty-five interviews in "Mature Artists" and "The New Generation," but have selected the most representative and, to our way of thinking, the most interesting. We arranged the order of the interviews not to establish particular cohorts, which would impose an arbitrary order on a particularly anarchic scene, but to establish some kind of narrative continuity, in that remarks made by one artist seemed to be continued or elaborated upon by the next. We should add here that all of the Estonian artists we interviewed, really nice people and wonderful artists, tried to be cooperative, but they were very reticent about answering our questions. As a result, we have not included any complete interviews we had with them, although some are mentioned and quoted when appropriate. A complete list of the interviewees is given at the end of the book. In the chapter titled "Conclusions," we summarize materials in the previous chapters. It will become clear that contradictions abound, not just about women's issues, but also about experiences in art school and in the ease or difficulty in exhibiting works. There is no single paradigmatic story and we acknowledge that fact throughout the pages of this book.

Before turning to the brief chronology and the interviews, we need a baseline from which to begin to measure the art of the 1990s. Surprisingly, we can use a famous poster created in the 1920s because of its still-contemporary relevance. In time, as new generations appear, its messages will grow less significant, but until then it visualizes modes of thought still difficult, we found, to overcome. Its title is *Lenin and the Female Worker* (*Every Kitchenmaid Must Be Able to Rule the State*) (fig. 1). One might think that it is a poster for women's liberation, and perhaps the artist and Soviet thinkers thought that it was. But if we study the images shown in the poster, we realize that it is not, and that it contains some big lies that to this day affect the way women think about their position in society. It is assumed, according to the poster, that women do menial and supportive work within a given range of occupations in order to aid their men in planning and building the new society. But no men are shown encouraging

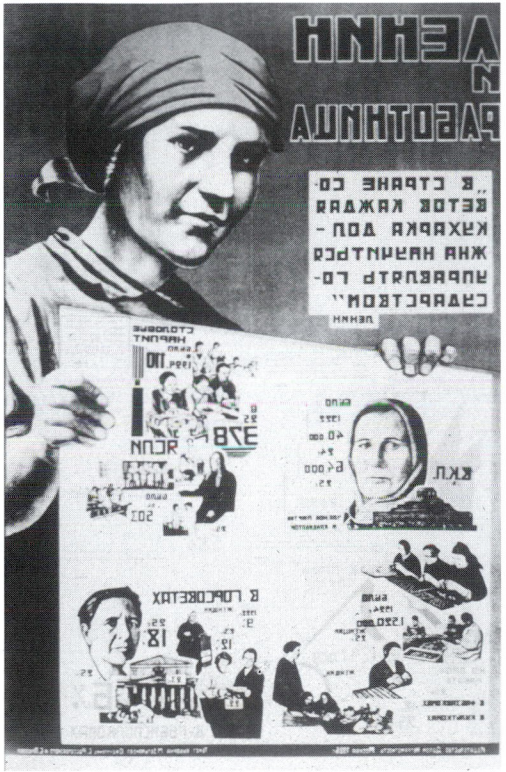

1. Anonymous, *Lenin and the Female Worker* (*Every Kitchenmaid Must Be Able to Rule the State*), ca. 1920s, poster. (Collection unknown.)

women or working beside them. Men simply do not work in the kitchen. Also, encoded in this poster is the notion that working for the state has priority over looking pretty, feminine, or womanly. The kerchiefs and no-nonsense features of the women desexualize them. It is as if they should become like men or look like men or think of themselves as male workers. They should subvert and deny their female specificity, their experiences as women both biologically and socially. They should become producers in the workforce. Equality is suggested—everybody should work—but at the same time women are encouraged to work in gender-suggested occupations—here as kitchenmaids.

It is difficult to believe, while walking the streets of Moscow and St. Petersburg on a summer's day in 2000 and seeing shockingly lithe, young women flaunting their seemingly sprayed-on clothing, that this poster could still have any resonance. In fact it is the other side of the same coin, since these young women are imitating all of those sexualized images one sees in contemporary Russian advertisements that appeal to the male gaze and to male fantasy. These young women, like their older sisters, are still not free from male domination. The poster is the groundline for what follows.

Brief Chronology

BECAUSE nobody kept an account of events, exhibitions, or conferences, it is virtually impossible to establish a precise chronology of the history of a feminist art or of the development of a woman's subject matter in art in the post-Soviet era. There is no archive. Some artists told us about some exhibitions, but their memories were very vague. They could not remember the exact year, who participated, and if there was an overarching theme. Some could remember participating in an exhibition with other women, but that there was no feminist agenda. So we have not tried to reconstruct a chronology except in the most general terms.

What is clear, however, is this: in the years initially following the establishment of the first democratic government in the history of Russia, artists were more concerned with their newly found freedom to exhibit without any constraint. Exploring feminist themes was decidedly less important than the sheer pleasure and exultation derived from showing works for the first time without the heavy burdens of censorship. In any event, feminism was little known around 1990 and largely misunderstood, and as a result, when artists and critics did turn to women's issues or women's subject matter, they did so sometimes with disdain and even with a mocking spirit. Most artists were much more excited by the fact that they could travel to the West for the first time. Westerners, able to travel east, created an entirely new situation in which artists for the first time were able to sell their works freely on the open market and make more money than they had ever imagined. If ever there was a euphoric moment in Russian and east European art after World War II, it occurred in the very early 1990s. Then, soon after, the Russian economy faltered and foreign collectors, the novelty having worn off, grew less interested in purchasing art. Within Russia, the

"New Russians" did not buy art and could not be counted on to support artists who were no longer employed by the government. As a result, through the middle years of the decade, artists were barely able to survive. Feminism, as artists told us, was considered a divisive issue at this time and a less important one than putting food on the table. There was some recovery, but then the bottom dropped out during the economic downturn in the summer of 1998.

At least one stalwart, Natalia Kamenetskaia, persisted in her goal of bringing feminist concerns to the Russian art world (see interview). With others she formed Idioma, founded in 1989 as an independent association of women pursuing careers in science, art, and literature. It also sponsored the first Russian feminist art magazine, also named *Idioma,* which appeared only once, as part of volume 7 of the American journal *Heresies* in 1992. Since then, Kamenetskaia has been involved in founding INO (the Russian acronym for Art [Iskusstvo], Science [Nauka], and Education [Obrazovanie]), which includes in its program the creation of a Contemporary Women's Art Museum, and the sponsorship a variety of exhibitions and conferences. It is even planning, with the State Tretiakov Gallery in Moscow in 2002, to sponsor an exhibition of women artists in Russian art, an exhibition unimaginable twelve, even five, years earlier. It will symbolically mark the arrival of a feminist movement in the Russian art world. With the changes in attitudes and perceptions through the decade, especially in its later years, artists such as Tatiana Nazarenko and Natalia Nesterova (both born in the 1940s; see interview with the former) have grown more important as role models or mother figures for younger artists intent on bringing their vision to and insisting on their place in the current art scene. What follows is a brief list of some of the exhibitions that are part of the history of a feminist art in post-Soviet Russia.

Around 1990, a handful of artists made and exhibited works that related directly to women's horizons and experiences. It was as if a visual documentation of the quotidian needed to be established and the ordinary needed to be celebrated. Such works reflected, it would seem, a pent-up desire to commemorate, even solemnize, individual experiences of no special import (this is not to say of no significant import), but which at the same time were shared by many women. The husband-and-wife team the Peppers (Ludmila Skripina [b. 1965] and Oleg Petrenko [b. 1964]), made assemblages around the theme of food (for example, *Bone Marrow,* 1989, which included pea-filled porcelain pipes and an apron) as well as two-dimensional images "scientifically" documenting women's bodily functions (also in 1989) as comments on the state of Soviet medical research

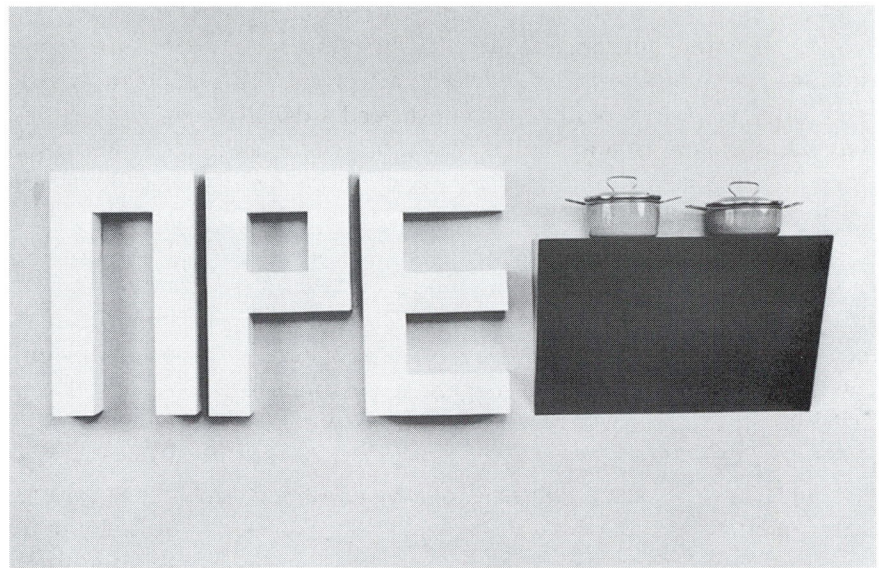

2. Elena Elagina, *PRE (Wonderful)*, 1990, installation with pans. (Courtesy Elena Elagina.)

and the barbaric treatment women still receive when having abortions. Elena Elagina (b. 1949; see interview), at about the same time and continuing for a few years, made assemblages also critiquing outdated medical procedures and conditions. In addition, in 1991, she also made a piece in which linked sausages are draped in the form of a rosary over a cross, a work that comments on a basic food as well as the availability of religious souvenirs in Russia. Other works neither glorify nor interrogate, but rather present for display kitchen artifacts (fig. 2). Some of her constructions were based on a safety manual for handling food-processing equipment distributed in the 1950s.[1] Other artists who used food and food-related images to comment on women's roles in Soviet society include Olga Chernisheva (b. 1962), who around 1990 based works on *The Book of Wholesome Food,* a popular cookbook during the Stalin era, in which, focusing on close-ups of hands working with kitchen equipment, she illustrated ways to make complex recipes for which ingredients were usually unavailable.

Into the middle years of the decade, Moscow-based Nina Kotyel (b. 1949) also explored household objects, particularly images of food (fig. 3). In particular, she painted large-scaled fruits, vegetables, bones, and glassware that dominate the pictorial surfaces. She told us that she uses

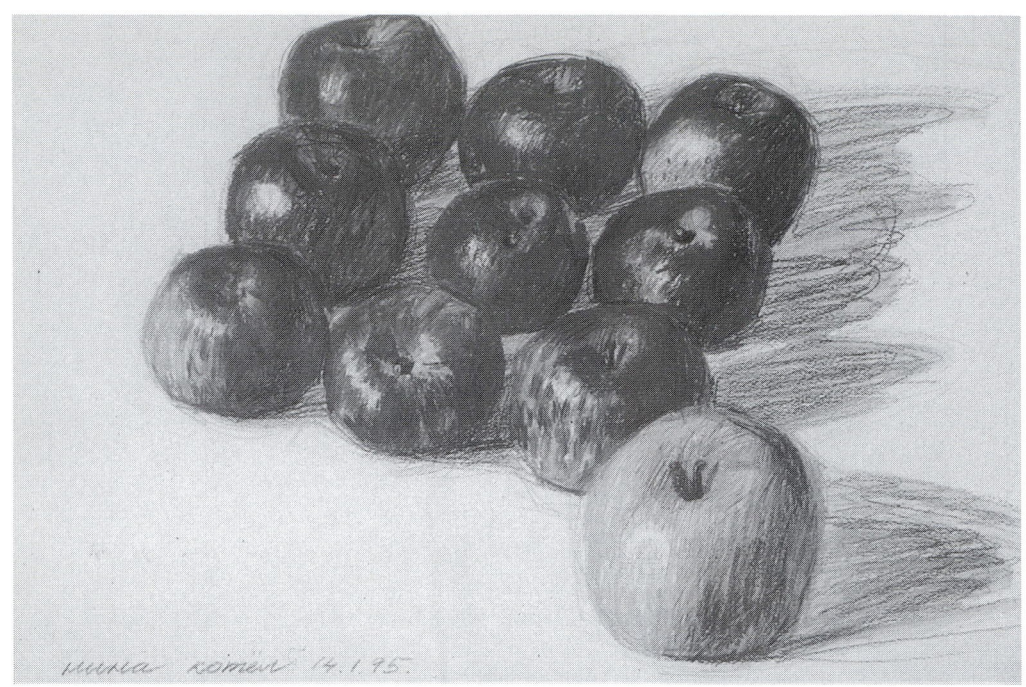

3.   Nina Kotyel, *Fruits,* ca. 1995, pastel on paper. (Courtesy Nina Kotyel.)

items she looks at, cooks, and eats every day. She feels that her work has a pop art quality, but irony is not her intention. Instead, she heroizes the objects that she, as a woman, deals with on a daily basis. Kotyel also finds mystery in their shapes. A pumpkin, for example, is large, closed, and, to her, enigmatic. It tells us nothing, but it seems to represent another world, a world of daydreams. It is as if the riddle of the Sphinx can be replicated in an ordinary kitchen, the world to which the average Russian woman is confined for several hours a day.

Several exhibitions were held early in the decade that were devoted to women as well as to notions of feminism. A few reveal the extent to which Russians misunderstood, honestly or not, the tenets of the movement. We also found that the exact chronology of the exhibitions is impossible to establish either from the literature or from personal memories. The exhibitions begin with a retrospective in 1989 titled *Women in Art,* dedicated to female students of Kazimir Malevich and Pavel Filonov, members of the Russian avant-garde early in the century. The second, concerned with textiles in art, was held in two parts, in Moscow and in St. Petersburg, in 1989–1990. The St. Petersburg show was titled *Text-Veiled Art.* We think the

Moscow version was titled *ZEN: Women as Subject and Object in Art* (*zen* is a contraction of *zhenstchina,* the Russian word for woman). In 1990, an exhibition titled *Clever Little Hands* took place in St. Petersburg. In the same year, a show titled *Femininity and Power* was presented in Moscow. And, finally, The *Woman Worker* opened in Moscow, also in 1990.[2]

The first exhibition, *Women in Art,* was curated by Olesya Turkina and Viktor Mazin, who also curated *Text-Veiled Art.* The latter show consisted of a collection of paintings on textiles by both men and women. All works were signed with female pseudonyms, and the public was invited to guess which works were done by men and which by women. The test here was to see if men created differently from women even though painting on textiles is considered a decorative-arts medium and is therefore associated with women. The premise was a specious one, since artists knew in advance the purpose of the exhibition and therefore might have entered totally uncharacteristic works. Further, women painters, most of whom were trained by male teachers, might have developed styles in emulation of their mentors so that innate female characteristics (assuming they might exist) were probably squelched years before. (We did ask in the interviews if one could tell the difference between a male and a female artist's work. The answers varied from a firm yes to an equally firm no.) And, finally, this exhibition in no way addressed issues of womanhood or the position of women in Russian society or in the Russian art world. It was, essentially, a cheap shot.

The part of this exhibition that was held in Moscow was curated by Valery Sergey. More men than women participated. Themes around which the paintings were organized included "Women and History," "Women and Politics," and "Women and Sex"; these were assigned by the male curator and therefore nullified any representation of categories women might have suggested and preferred. Here, the premise was clearly that women paint subjects, perhaps a bit differently but still the same subjects, that men prefer to paint. The exhibition *Femininity and Power,* was organized by Oleg Kulik, who literally hung the show on dress hangers. Whatever the justification, the effect reinforced the dismissal of women's art as just that— women's art or dressmaker's art.

In 1990, seven artists participated in *The Woman Worker,* probably the first exhibition devoted exclusively to women's issues, interests, and experiences. The artists were Anna Alchuk (see interview), Elena Elagina, Sabina Hengsem, Vera Khlebnikova, Maria Konstantinova, Irina Nakhova, and Alena Shakohovskaia. (Elagina, Khlebnikova, and Nakhova did not discuss this show in their interviews.) Elagina did tell us that she remembered another show around this time in which Joseph Bakshtein, now director of the Institute of Contemporary Art in Moscow, curated a show of women artists in which he surreptitiously exhibited his own work and that of Konstantin Zvezdochetov.

Two exhibitions dating from 1995 in which art critic Maria Katkova participated reveal the ambiguities and conflicts concerning feminism that people still held in the middle of the decade. The first show was really an antifeminist or antiwoman kind of exhibition that had as a subtheme the self-abasement of women; the second, to the contrary, was a good example of calling attention to the domestic chores women face daily. Her comments led us to believe, when we spoke with her in 1995, that she had not yet fully digested the tenets of feminism or entirely understood its program even though she acknowledged quite knowingly that Russians misunderstand feminism for all the wrong reasons—seeing feminists as ill-mannered monsters, neutered women opposed to heterosexual relations, virtual men killers, and unable to differentiate between socially gendered constructions and physiology. We think, and this has been corroborated by several Russian women in the past year or two, that the same kinds of confusions abound today as well.

Concerning the first exhibition, Katkova saw nothing wrong with encouraging the artist Sergei Miturich to hold an exhibition based on an imaginary character he had invented. This was a fictitious women artist named Lubov Solokhova who had a "documented" past in the Russian art world, including membership in the artists' union. She was supposed to have visited London many years ago, and while there had seen several calling cards for prostitutes in telephone booths. She then brought them back to Russia and Miturich, using a female pseudonym for himself, decided to have an exhibition. He placed the calling cards against a wall carefully designed to look like a London street, as if they had been photographed on the spot. Miturich justified his activities by saying that he wanted to enter a woman's mind and psyche. (A prostitute's, no less, speaking of the prerogatives of patriarchy.) The press was not told of the ruse when the exhibition opened, but a critic, Andrei Kovalev, revealed Miturich's machinations by arguing that women would have objected to another woman doing a show about prostitutes and their calling cards.

The other exhibition was called *Bon Appétit*. It dealt with the problems women face in obtaining provisions. Katkova likened housewives to huntresses, running from one store to another, carrying heavy bags. Men, she said, just don't care about such things; They come home from work, eat, and go to sleep. In the performance piece, she invited a male friend to sit and eat for an hour before an audience. He was instructed to eat slowly and to eat everything put before him. At first, he was embarrassed, she said, and then a look of horror came into his eyes. Journalists present started to laugh and then began to feel sorry for him. She then said, "Imagine what women have to go through every day." Her purpose was to make men aware of how long it takes to get the food and to put in on the table. The performance ended with a lengthy discussion of women's domestic chores.

According to Alla Mitrofanova, a critic from St. Petersburg (see interview), there were more small, marginal organizations in her city than in Moscow—a feminist club, a gender center, a gay group whose members were aware of each other—through the middle years of the decade. Toward the end of the decade, despite the economic reversals, feminist awareness spread in both cities concerning gender issues as well as the needs of women, and, equally important in a country where there are very few art magazines and exchanges of information are hard to come by, networking between groups in both cities has obviously begun. Concerns about homosexuality, cross-dressing, and transgendering have also been increasingly acknowledged in the art world. These issues were brought together in two significant exhibitions in 1999 in both cities, *Gender Boundaries* and *Anamnesis lapsus memoriae (Remembrances Are the Mistakes of Memory),* sponsored by the INO Creative Workshop Center (Center of Contemporary Women's Art Program) in Moscow and the Cyber-Femin-Club in St. Petersburg. Unlike the exhibitions in these two cities around 1990, these were presented in a much more serious, knowing, and advocative way. (Of the eighteen artists whose works were shown, we were able to interview eleven.)

Kamenetskaia, in a take-no-prisoners statement, said in the exhibition catalogue, "The male curators, art critics, and all other men eager to climb the sacred Mount Olympus prefer to believe that in terms of "Big Scale" Art THERE ISN'T ANY 'WOMAN'S ART.' It doesn't exist as a species. Period. A woman artist—if her art is addressed to WOMEN as well as to men—is no ARTIST. Art cannot be divided on the basis of gender—but only if this gender happens to be female."[3] Anna Alchuk's entry represents the aggressive posture of the exhibitors (fig. 4; see interview). Her piece, six photographs of men in the pose of the Venus de Milo, are objects of contemplation. At their center, she included a plaster copy of the head of Venus who, instead of being the object of contemplation, now contemplates the male body. Other works address issues of cross-dressing and are intended to challenge

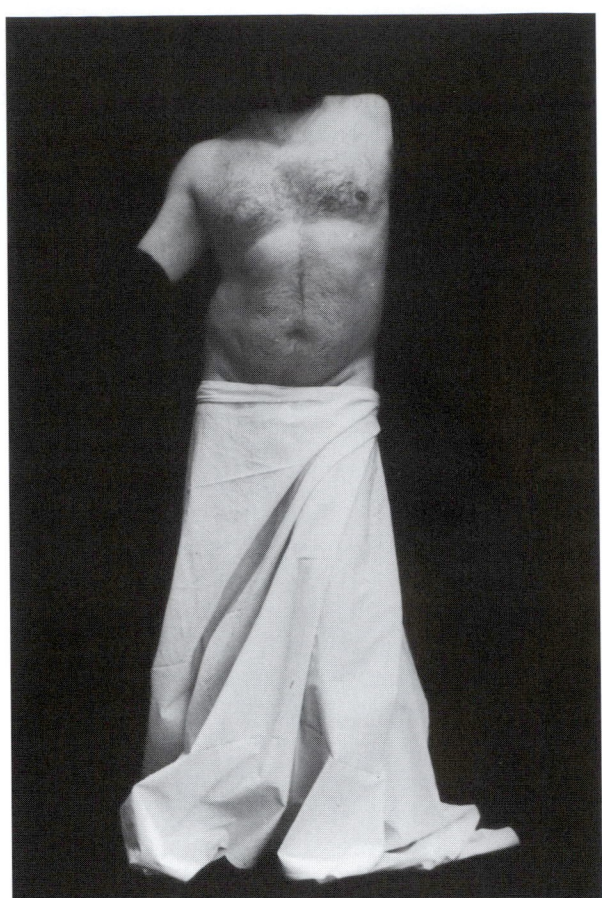

4. Anna Alchuk, *A Girl's Toy*, 1995, photograph. (Courtesy Anna Alchuk.)

. . . .

socially constructed gender roles (see interview with Ludmila Gorlova). It is interesting to note here that some interviewees had referred to the marginalized presence of male homosexual and lesbian art in ways that denied its significance. Now, such art is being seen and, more important, read as an important challenge to traditional ways of viewing gender differences and therefore is now accepted as bearing quite directly on feminist concerns. With organizations now in place in Moscow and St. Petersburg (we do not know the situation in other cities), the hope is, on the part of the participants, that their voices will be heard and understood.

A note here. In the interviews, some artists remembered a few exhibitions so vaguely that we did not include them here. Nor did we include in this chapter discussion of Alena Martinova's video presentations of her own nude body during the mid-1990s (see interview), which we believe in retrospect helped create a climate of acceptance for the presentation of the body, especially the nude body, later in the decade. The reason is that the list would be entirely too fragmentary. We think it is more important to get a sense of the changing attitudes from the beginning of the decade to its end.

Mature Artists

WE INCLUDE in this section artists born in the 1920s, 1930s, and 1940s, as well as those who achieved recognition in the 1970s. Their comments and their work serve as background to the developments of the 1990s. Nevertheless, in their remarks about their art school training, their careers, and their family life, they made observations and recounted experiences that for many still hold true today. Some, like Dzemma Skulme in Latvia and Tatiana Nazarenko and Natalia Nesterova in Moscow were singled out by younger artists as role models because of their strong personalities, the positions they held, and the quality of their work.

Vera Dreznina

Vera Dreznina (b. 1924) was the most senior artist we interviewed. A realist and primarily a portraitist, she was clearly able to survive the worst years of Stalin's rule by painting works that did not offend the authorities. Although any discussion of feminism or feminist art was not part of her way of thinking, she did recall certain experiences that contemporary artists have also encountered. She did mention one thing, almost too casually, that emphasizes the break with the past that took place during the Stalinist years. She said that Aleksander Mickhailovich Gerasimov (1881–1963), who headed the Organizing Committee of the Union of Soviet Artists from 1939 to 1957 and was president of the USSR Academy of Arts from 1947 to 1957, had several older teachers arrested, thus ending their teaching careers and the links their students might have had to earlier generations of artists. On occasion, younger artists told us that an old, revered figure was still allowed to teach, usually in provincial cities, but seeing and studying avant-garde works was virtually impossible, and discussion of unapproved art was dangerous.

RB: Tell me about yourself.

VD: I was born in Moscow in 1924. I entered art school in 1937. We had some famous teachers, but Gerasimov decided to clean up the place and had many arrested. I finished at the Surikov Art Institute in 1950. We were three girls and thirty boys. Today, emancipation is arriving in Russia, but most of our women still think of themselves as a *baba* (old woman, hag). In Russia, a woman was never anything else but a *baba*.

RB: And earlier?

VD: It was different then. We had many emancipated women. But we had to accept what we were told.

RB: Who were your teachers?

VD: Men. We had no women teachers. There was one woman who organized a school, but could not teach in it. She protested to some ministers, but then she disappeared.

RB: Did you have time for your own work then?

VD: No. I never had enough time. One artist I met [Alexander Vasilevich] Kuprin [1880–1960], told me never to get married if I want to be an artist. [Dreznina is now a grandmother.] But I became a popular artist. A portrait of Pushkin won a prize and the Pushkin Museum in St. Petersburg bought it. I received many official commissions after that. I was straight as an arrow. My work is realistic and I never made waves. My mother, of course, was a great help. She dedicated herself to my family.

RB: Do you think it is easier now for women?

VD: I never considered the question. The generation after mine is different, of course. Artists like Tatiana Nazerenko [see interview] and Natalia Nesterova have a different mentality from mine. They rule the world. They and others are daring, tough-minded. In my time, boys were always considered like gods, but not girls. But I think today the women of Russia are more important, have more clout and more self-esteem than men. Even though men don't acknowledge this, women are better.

In a statement in a catalogue of her work, Dreznina made very clear the situation that all interviewees acknowledged and with which they struggled, some by working within and around its strictures, others by rejecting it completely.

It's generally known that a family is a distraction for a painter trying to sit in a studio, or work in fresh air. When an artist is male, then all work about the house is done by his wife. But a woman artist has got all house work with her. These things are difficult to combine, especially when you love your family and work as well.[1]

Ratios of men and women artists, or boy and girl students, varied in the memories of interviewees. It would appear that some recounted to us their school days (there were special grade schools and high schools for gifted students), and others remembered their years in art academies or institutes. A general consensus would be that there were usually more girl students in the lower grades and more boy students at the institutes. Teachers often discouraged women from pursuing a career in the fine arts, as opposed to the decorative arts, since many dropped out to marry and have children.

Dzemma Skulme

Dezma Skulme (b. 1925) is an abstract painter from Latvia who graduated from the Latvian Academy of Arts (fig. 5). After serving as deputy chair and secretary of the Latvian Union of Artists, she became chair in 1982 and, in effect, has served as a mother figure for many artists. As she and other artists from the Baltic countries made clear, in their countries, in comparison to the Soviet Union, there were many more woman artists relative to the number of male artists. Artists comparable in age to Skulme told us that they had memories of freedom and independence before the Soviets annexed their countries in 1940, and because of their greater proximity to the West as well as the availability of Western books and magazines that arrived from Poland, they had easier access to Western art and Western ideas than Russian artists. Nevertheless, and even though many had traveled abroad in the 1990s, all of the interviewees from these countries held traditional ideas about male-female relationships. One or two had been to feminist conferences, but exposure to the various ideas put forth at least initially dumbfounded some and were ignored by others. We interviewed Skulme twice. The following interview dates from 1995.

RB: Did you ever experience discrimination?
DS: Never in my art, but I did in daily life. My mother was an artist and she experienced discrimination in the 1920s. She was a sculptor, won prizes, but lost commissions because she was a woman. In my own time, many women became artists after the Khrushchev thaw in the late 1950s. Perhaps this was a result of the loss of so many men in the war. In any event, in those days men were more repressed than women. They

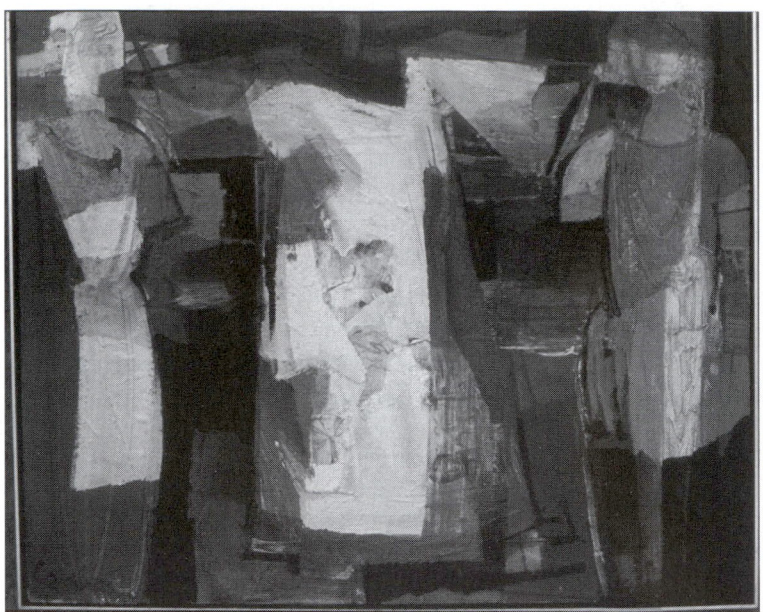

5. Dzemma Skulme, *Caryatids*, 1986, oil with ink and graphite on canvas. (Courtesy Jane Voorhees Zimmereli Art Museum, Rutgers, the State University of New Jersey. The Norton and Nancy Dodge Collection of Nonconformist Art from the Soviet Union. Copyright © 2001 Artists Rights Society [ARS}, New York/AKKA-LAA, Riga.)

were hounded and accused of all sorts of things, while we were left alone by the authorities. We were able to keep up our folk traditions in the arts when the men went to war.

RB: Tell me about your schooling.

DS: I finished gymnasium [secondary school] in 1933 and the Latvian Academy of Arts in 1949. In art school, the women were better, the stronger men having probably already emigrated. The competition was stiff for entry, but the women worked harder and were more responsible. Yet at the academy, men received more attention. I was always shown respect. People would tell me that I was their queen. I was lucky. The Soviets, of course, claimed that women had equality. That was nonsense. There were more women teachers in the schools because the pay was too little for a man to support a family.

RB: Who supported you?

DS: My husband. He, too, was an artist and had very progressive ideas.

RB: Is there anything to the notion that people can tell a woman's painting from a man's?

DS: I have to think about that, but sometimes I look at my work and think it lacks toughness. Perhaps women lack a certain logic and toughness.

RB: So you are saying that your work is more delicate and you would like it to be more masculine.

DS: Yes. I aim for that. Inwardly, I feel that I don't want to express something feminine because I know that it becomes more moving and emotional. I always have to include masculine power in my works. On the other hand, my husband, who died in 1983, said that his work lacked emotional content. I do believe that a woman is more sensitive and emotional, even more diplomatic. She is always seeking connections between opposite sides.

RB: Do you have any thoughts on feminist debates on essentialism and cultural formation?

DS: We haven't even begun to think of such things. But I remember a few years ago there was a feminist conference in Riga. I saw it on TV. Some women who were high officials from Sweden and Finland were having a dialogue with some of our ministers. When the Scandinavian women began to ask questions, I blushed and was embarrassed by our men. It was very obvious that they were condescending. The men began to use old-fashioned, flirtatious language and made asses of themselves. I thought to myself, "My God! How come I didn't think about this sooner?" Then I began to realize that I feel discrimination in my own house. For example, my son-in-law is a theologian and is a very nice person. Ours is a big house and we all live together. Do you think he ever helps out around here? Instead, he'll tell me what to do. My son is an artist and he, too, does not help his wife. Who needs a husband? I could use a wife, myself.

The repression of men, mentioned by Skulme, was also described by other interviewees. The line of thought went something like this. The Soviet state repressed everybody, but especially men, more of whom were sent to Siberia or died in war. In addition, since many of their teachers were women, they had been robbed, to a certain extent, of their masculinity as children. All this contributed to weaknesses in their character and their inability to stand up to authority. But, men, in turn, dominated women in the professional and domestic spheres. Therefore, everybody experienced some kind of repression. With regard to male-female relationships, it is clear that the older women, unlike their younger sisters and daughters, accept their lot without too much visible concern—as if to say with a shrug, "This is the way things are. What's the problem?"

Malda Muizule

Malda Muizule (b. 1937) is Latvian. Her comments on a woman artist's life were typical of those of other women of her generation. Although she often paints nudes, she had no special reason for doing so. This interview was given in 1995.

MM: I graduated from the Latvian Academy of Arts in 1963. We painted from classical models, so I don't paint kolkhoz women.

RB: This was allowed even though the Soviets did not like the painting of nudes?

MM: Compared to Russia, we had more freedom. In my work, women have curved lines (fig. 6). My husband, who is also an artist, would probably use straight lines. Our women artists paint from inner feelings. A man would just say that he is going to make such and such a picture, and then do it. I can't say anything like that. I have to get into the mood of the picture. My husband is always planning what he is going to paint, whereas I can only think of what I will do at the moment.

RB: Are women artists treated the same way as male artists?

MM: A man has more of an inclination to become an official, but that does not mean he is better. Our time is more limited, since we have families. We are the ones who take care of everything. I have always been the nurturer. After I had my children I grew more self-confident in my art because I had to work at great speed in between preparing meals, getting the children to school, and all of that. I tried to save at least two hours a day for my art, and I found that I could do it. Otherwise, I would have been unhappy with myself. I have friends who stopped painting, but I would not do that.

RB: Is your husband supportive?

MM: Yes, but at first I didn't think he respected me as an artist. He never actually said anything, but it felt that way. For the past twenty years, I have been the one sought after. I gained recognition. Then he understood that perhaps I had God's gift in that I was able to switch from peeling potatoes to painting pictures.

RB: How about your schooling?

MM: There was no differentiation between boys and girls. Nobody had special privileges.

RB: Do you have support groups here?

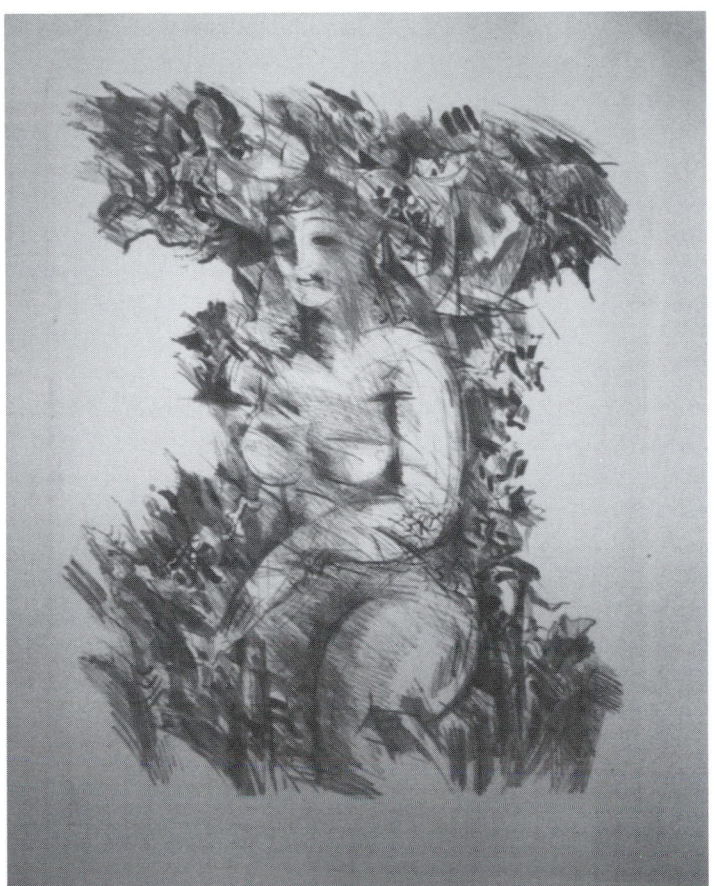

6. Malda Muizule, *Nude*, ca. 1993, watercolor. (Courtesy Malda Muizule.)

MM: No. If there were, they would be unusual. Once in Sweden, I attended a feminist get-together of Swedish and Latvian women. They were academics and I did not like what they said about men. They said that our men are the worst, that they don't help their wives. But that's not true. We're used to doing all the work. This is how it has always been. You can't change that. I told the women that the most important thing is that a man should be a man. We need them around the house to fix things that we cannot fix. Besides, I think our men are rather fine people. I also don't want my husband in the kitchen. He wouldn't be able to do anything, anyway, except spoil things. The feminists in Sweden also said that a woman should occupy the financial ministry. They said that women always manage the finances in the house and that the laws men have established don't work well. I couldn't believe such educated women could say such things.

RB: Do women think differently from men?

MM: Very differently. A woman would never invent a machine gun. All the means of destruction have been created by men. Women have strong maternal feelings and bear children, which is a creative act. Women work all the time, and want to do good. I believe women don't have an instinct for great evil. Our human history has always been dependent on men. That's why we have so much destruction. I can even see it in my husband. All men are attracted to guns and rockets. I tell him [my husband] not to paint a picture with a gun in it. I could never paint such a picture. I can't stand painting something that is horrible and ugly. There is so much horror in life and I don't want to add to it. I want to make beautiful pictures that will give a person pleasure and hope.

RB: What if women had controlled history?

MM: We might have scratched each other's eyes out, but we would never be so destructive. Men don't use swords just for self-defense. Aggression is the thing that differentiates men from women. A while ago, I heard a woman who spoke in abstractions about our rights. Well, I thought there were laws to take care of all that, but unfortunately our basic biological differences do not allow us to use those rights.

Muizule and others made clear that since they had survived the war and the Soviet occupation and are currently managing to get through the constant economic turbulence of the post-Soviet years, they would survive without feminism—whatever that term meant to them. They feel themselves to be strong and resourceful, but as Anita Meldere, in the following interview, said, they do not have much energy left for a fight with men. They all acknowledged that men were different from women biologically. This could not be denied. And they also acknowledged that men had certain social privileges, but these caused no severe strains and provoked no cause for action. What in the West would be perceived as discrimination was accepted as normal by women such as Muizule and Meldere.

Anita Meldere

Anita Meldere (b. 1940s) lives in Riga and paints in a realistic style. This interview was given in 1995.

AM: In art school, we were all equal. But in life, women are different. Women are the softer gender and experience things on a deeper level than men. Women are more sensitive and have roots in nature. A women will reflect her life in her work. I have a child and a strong need for family life, but at the same time I love art. The main thing for me is not to lose time from painting, for which I never have enough time. But there is always conflict. You cannot devote yourself fully to art and to your family. I believe that all this is reflected in women's paintings. Male artists can devote all their time to their work. It is probably biological. If a woman works outside the home, people look askance at her.

RB: What about schooling at the academy?

AM: We were all treated equally. Talent was all that mattered.

RB: Were women, then, in positions as high as those of the men?

AM: No. The academy was run by men. When I applied for a teaching position, it was made clear that male students were pushed ahead of me. I then taught preparatory courses and I am ranked as a senior teacher, not a professor. I teach night courses to young people in a three-year program, after which they enter the academy. I could never become a professor, whereas men in my class have been awarded that rank.

RB: Would you ever contest that?

AM: I don't think so. I'm too tired. To struggle requires energy and heroics. A long time ago, I decided to do what suits me best.

RB: What effect did it have to see your male colleagues assume higher positions?

AM: On the human level, it was hurtful and demeaning. It lowered my self-esteem. But, you know, you can't do anything about it. So you keep quiet.

RB: Is the situation better now?

AM: Things could be a lot better, especially more medical attention for women.

RB: You paint nudes.

AM: The human body has always been of great interest to me. You can enter the human spirit through the body. We had male models in school, but I rarely paint male nudes now. Not many male models want to sit for me. I think a nude male is afraid to be stared at by women, and I am not sure that a man would trust a woman artist, anyway. But with women subjects I can establish mood, express my feelings, and my experiences with, for example, the aging process. A man would be more rational. Also, a man might look at a nude female model as a woman. I tend to see her from a formal perspective.

Meldere's offhanded comment about the lack of medical attention for women and her inability to link that with feminist concerns represents a point of view still prevalent at least among the more mature artists with whom we spoke. They feel that some government program might someday take care of a problem when the economic situation improves, but then again there might never be such a program. There obviously is no tradition for grassroots organization, and its importance in the face of male (or governmental) inertia just does not occur to them—since they also still believe that there was and is equality. They do not see coalescing around women's issues as a possibility. Feminism means something else to them—something strange, perhaps a menace to their lifestyles, an imported ideology from western Europe and the United States that has no relevance to their lives.

Estonian artists were even more reticent than Latvians about discussing feminist issues. Many had never given them a thought. The principal reason seems to be that since there are so many women artists in their country, they cannot imagine the existence of any kind of discrimination. In addition, many women are art critics and run galleries, and a woman is director of the national museum. One or two took offense when we asked about discrimination, thinking that we might assume that their men would mistreat their women. Another made very clear that they were northern people, not Slavs like the Russians, and that we should not assume that Estonian men treat women in the same way as Russians. However, they too, like the Latvians, were not bothered by the fact that there were usually more female students yet more male teachers in the art schools. Of the Estonian artists we interviewed, Vive Tolli (b. 1928), Concordia Klar (b. 1930s), Silvi Liiva (b. 1940s), Malle Leis (b. 1940s), Liina Siib (b. 1940s), Regina Lukk (b. 1940s), Sirje Runge (b. 1940s), and Marje Uksine (b. 1950s), only Uksine, a graphics artist, displayed any anger about her situation (fig. 7). When asked if she was ever mistreated, she said, "I always feel it. I am not considered as serious as a man. I worked for a while as an art editor for a publisher, and felt that if I were a man, I would have had an easier time socially. I felt perhaps I should have been a man"; and then assuming blame for her own situation, she said, "Or perhaps it's just me." Only one or two Russian women expressed such strong feelings about preferring to be a man, no doubt prompted by the treatment they had received or by having allowed themselves to be manipulated into such self-doubts. In either instance, they accepted the false premise that the victim is guilty of the crime. This suggested to us that since virtually all interviewees saw themselves as strong women, only the psychologically sturdy can survive as artists in eastern Europe.

But it is not so simple. Subjugating one's individuality and therefore one's sense of self-worth in face of communal cooperation was part of the Soviet ideological baggage. In addition, all of the Latvian and Estonian art-

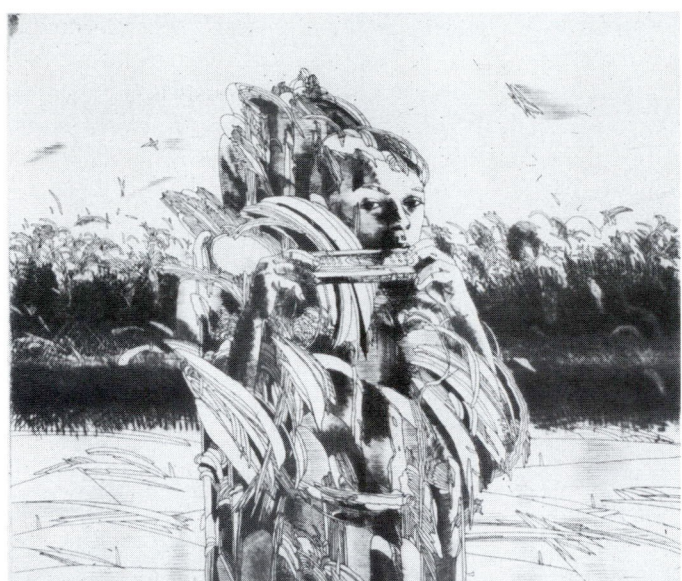

7. Marje Uksine, *Recollection*, 1986, etching. (Courtesy Jane Voorhees Zimmerli Art Museum, Rutgers, The State University of New Jersey. The Norton and Nancy Dodge Collection of Nonconformist Art from the Soviet Union.)

ists who had matured during Soviet times felt that they had been occupied by a hated and repressive foreign power. The Russians and their local henchmen were the enemy, not men in general. Repression and guilt derived as much if not more from political sources as from personal relationships. Similar feelings were either implied or expressed in even stronger terms by women dissident artists in the Soviet Union who viewed the authorities as their enemy. Valentina Kropivnitskaia (b. 1924), one of the first women dissident artists, made this point over and over again when we spoke with her at her home in Paris in 1995 and on subsequent occasions in New York (fig. 8). Not surprisingly, she has insisted that she was always treated as an equal by her fellow artists (in the eyes of the authorities she was as much an enemy as the male dissidents) and that no difference exists between the art of men and women.

In St. Petersburg, we interviewed three women of comparable age, Ludmila Kutzenko, Valentina Pivovarova, and another who would not give her name, all born in the 1920s, or perhaps the last two in the early 1930s. All three were abstract painters who had studied at the Mukhin Institute of Industrial Arts and with Vladimir Sterligov (1904–1973), a teacher and

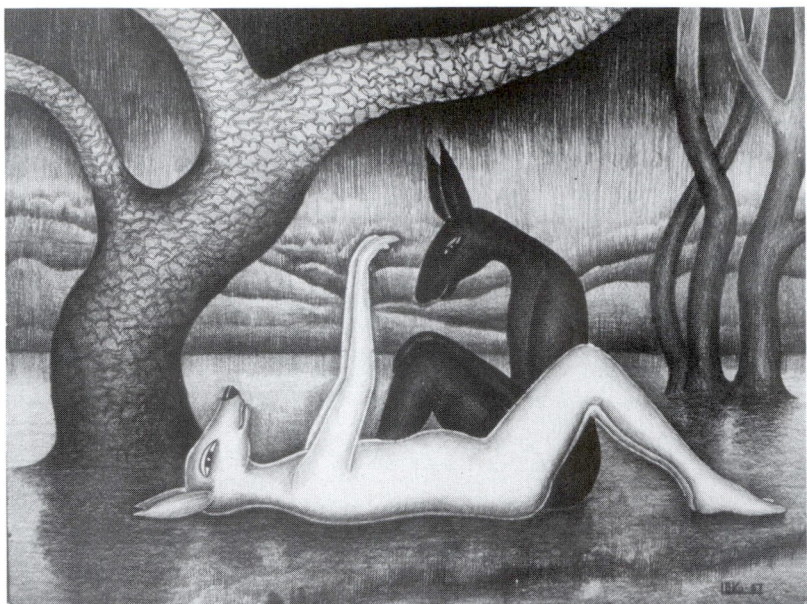

8. Valentina Kropivnitskaia, *White and Black Beasts,* 1967, graphite on paper. (Courtesy Jane Voorhees Zimmerli Art Museum, Rutgers, The State University of New Jersey. The Norton and Nancy Dodge Collection of Nonconformist Art from the Soviet Union.)

something of a guru who had managed to teach about and have his students paint abstract works even though the authorities disapproved. They answered questions interchangeably and essentially in the same voice, and gave us some idea about life and personal attitudes in the 1940s. This interview dates from 1995.

Valentina Pivovarova

VP: One has to desire to be an artist more than life itself. If a woman concentrates on housework, then nothing will come of her dreams. Art for us is tied to our lives. Art is like a calling. [None of the three had ever married.]

RB: What was art school like?

VP: We were treated very well, except that some teachers [at the Mukhin Institute] would, with a wave of the hand, say that nothing would come of talented girls because they would get married. But basically our education was the same for boys and girls. From the start of the Revolution, we had equality. But it was always more difficult for women to enter schools of higher education, particularly the technical departments. We started our art training just after the war. Veterans were admitted first, and men usually won the competitions. But generally there was equality. But getting a good position was more difficult for women. Women could get better positions in crafts and applied-arts programs. In our painting classes, there might be one women to ten men. Inequality existed, but not on the surface. The three of us taught at the Mukhin Institute.

RB: Do you ever make paintings of men?

VP: No. Their pants are not very pretty. But we have done some monumental female figures.

RB: What do you think of male artists?

VP: Men are more rational and logical. Women are more flexible and emotional. One could take *flexible* to mean flighty, but I mean resourceful.

As with other interviewees, these three saw no inconsistency in saying that there was equality, but that men could get jobs more easily and that women were shunted off into the crafts and applied-arts fields. In effect, if everybody was taken care of in some way, then there really was equality, and if women were less intellectual and rational than men, then the applied arts was the right place for them. Besides, one cannot be a mother and an artist. Once again, "What is the problem?"

Natalia Zhilina

Natalia Zhilina (b. 1934), from St. Petersburg, was a dissident artist, but as much as she felt oppressed by the authorities, she also told us that male dissident artists did not necessarily view her as an equal. In her paintings, largely portraits and family scenes, she keys up her colors to a bright finish (fig. 9). This interview was given in 1995.

RB: Did you notice when you were a student how teachers treated students?

NZ: The attitude toward girls was that they would not produce anything good. In order to be noticed, a girl had to be very loud and draw attention to herself.

RB: Did you know dissident artists before the fall of Communism?

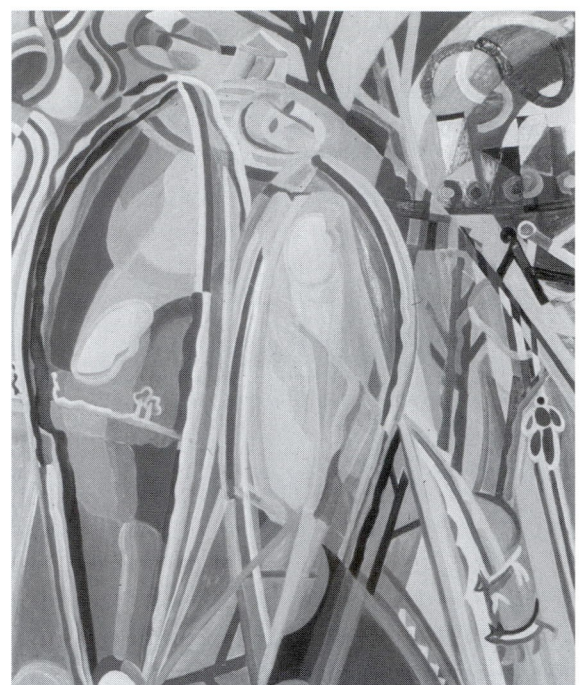

9. Natalia Zhilina, *Rae-guliai*, 1985–1986, oil on canvas. (Courtesy Jane Voorhees Zimmerli Art Museum, Rutgers, The State University of New Jersey. The Norton and Nancy Dodge Collection of Nonconformist Art from the Soviet Union.)

NZ: I knew all of them. When we were allowed to hold the very first open exhibition of dissident art in St. Petersburg in 1974 at the Gaz Palace, they did not contact me. That was really hurtful. I was, however, invited to a big exhibition in Moscow in 1975. I am now somewhat famous and I am part of a group called the Pushkinskaia. Nobody in the group would ever insult a woman, but the men my age are not very pleasant about it. The younger ones show more respect.

RB: Do you have a family?

NZ: Yes, my son, Mitia, is an artist [he organized the Mitki group in the mid-1980s] and so is my daughter, Maria [see interview with Maria Snigirovskaia]. I have a lot of energy. My mother helped me raise the children. My husband was not a help, and died after being institutionalized. I could not paint when he was around. He would scream that I belonged in the kitchen. People just didn't take women artists seriously.

RB: Do you think there is a difference between paintings by women and by men?

NZ: Yes, no matter how a woman tries to be tough in her work, there is still a softness. They have a need to express joy. Men like to suffer. They can't stand pain. Therefore, their pictures express tragedy, pathos. A woman is always searching for happiness. I believe the Lord has imbued the female soul with an élan vital. It is a gift to strive for happiness. Men want to destroy. Women want to make things whole. Men create with their brains, women with their hearts. My work is about the happiness of motherhood. I don't put men in my paintings except my son.

RB: Will you exhibit only with women?

NZ: No. I don't like separate exhibitions. I don't participate in women-only shows.

Zhilina raised some points that we heard repeatedly. First, women are the caregivers and men are often psychologically repressive, in that they do not respect women artists to the extent that they should, nor are they helpful in day-to-day activities. Second, women are more emotional and men more rational. Third, all-women exhibitions are frowned upon because they represent some kind of special pleading or admittance of second-rate status through the implication that the women involved are not good enough to exhibit with men. In respect to exhibitions, Zhilina and others also think in old-fashioned ways in that they have not yet fully grasped the fact that with government support no longer available, they are now independent entrepreneurs selling a product: their art. They, but not all, do not yet realize that exhibitions organized and hung in a professional manner might help marketability through exposure, or that interesting, feminist-generated subject matter or themes, or just the presence in one exhibition of several women artists regardless of their chosen themes, might generate enthusiastic responses. Finally, older women, to a greater extent than younger women, do not like to include male figures in their work.

Marina Elkonina (b. 1935), a Moscow-based sculptor of large abstract reliefs, corroborated Zhilina's remarks, adding that many women dropped out of art school before their graduation to have families or ceased to make art because of the time needed to stand in lines, buy food, prepare meals, and do all the other domestic chores. Elkonina also reiterated the point that, as a divorced mother, she raised and financially supported her child. Her former husband, like most others, offered no or little help regardless of the circumstances. She also mentioned that male art critics tended to be more sympathetic to male artists, that "being a woman did not help. In fact, it was a hindrance. The thought was that women should do something else, something less strenuous, more quiet, like housework. This was all out in the open, and it still is. Women have had a hard time breaking through. There never was equality." She also said that although she was not sure if she was a powerful woman, at least she had maintained her self-respect. This point was stated quite often. But this sense of self-ennobling has, so far, not led to any strong desire to organize in formal or informal ways to promote true equality, except among a small handful of women in the art world.

A few Russian artists in the 1970s and 1980s, because of their actions or the positions they held, have been acknowledged as formative influences on the younger women. It cannot be argued that there was a direct line of development between them and younger artists, but their presence, or at least some knowledge of their activities, helped provide a climate of opinion for women artists to create thoughtful and provocative works. But reflecting attitudes toward feminism early in the decade, the younger artists responded more as individuals than as part of a feminist movement. The older artists include Nonna Goriunova, Rimma Gerlovina, Tatiana Nazarenko, and Natalia Nesterova.

Nonna Goriunova (b. 1944) graduated from the Stroganov Art Institute in 1967, having completed the program in weaving and interior design. She credits her husband, the artist Francesco Infante (b. 1943), however, with convincing her to become an artist rather than to remain an applied artist, a rare inversion of the usual relationship within such marriages, in which competition often leads to divorce; to disparagement of the wife as a fine, rather than an applied, artist; or to both. Nevertheless, Goriunova insisted more than once that her priorities have always been to be a wife first, a mother second, and an artist third, and to apportion her time accordingly. On several occasions, she gave up art-making entirely for her family, saying to us that "so many families fall apart if you put your ambitions first. We have many unhappy women artists who lead lonely lives."

She and Infante were among the first to do what they called projects, which today would be called performances. These date from 1965. She acknowledges Infante as the leader, saying, "I never thought it should be otherwise." Perhaps her most important performance for our purposes was *Forest Ritual* of 1968, which took place in winter in a forest near Moscow. She and her husband had built a snow wall, and as candles melted an opening in the wall, Goriunova could be seen, posing naked.[2] Aside from its importance as an example of dissident art, this was, perhaps the first such flagrant challenge to the repression of the nude body in Soviet art. But in the context of dissident art, the piece was less an example of eroticism in art as it was an assertion on the part of a woman artist to reclaim her body from Soviet control, through which women were instructed to have babies and to work for the greater glory of the fatherland. Goriunova's act, in this context, was one of total independence. Furthermore, she presented herself not as a sex object, but as an image in a ritual within a particular performance. She acted on her own behalf, not in response to male demands or desires, and not to become the object of anybody's gaze. This desire, to reclaim control of one's own body from Soviet control, which is difficult for Westerners to understand, subsequently prompted art critic Alla Mitrofanova, who realized after the fall of the Soviet Union in the early 1990s that she was for the first time in control of her own destiny as well as her own body, to view childbirth for the first time as an existential, rather than as a biological and state-mandated, event (see interview).

In conversation, Goriunova also alluded to another kind of misunderstanding of feminism. It lies in confusing a feminist with a "monster woman." Virtually any woman who is a feminist, we heard several times, might be a monster woman. She is like a tank, figuratively and literally, who will stop for nothing and for nobody. She is probably an official and has lost most of her femininity. She represents the worst of the past and, if allowed to assume power, potentially the worst of the present and future as well. In time, this image will certainly grow less strong, but it still had great potency, and literal presence, at the end of the 1990s.

Rimma Gerlovina (b. 1951) left the Soviet Union and settled in New York in 1980, before the advent of feminism in her native country. But both she and her husband, Valerii (b. 1945) with whom she works closely, left their mark on the history of body art in Russia, especially through a series of published photographs of their performance piece titled *Zoo, March 1977,* executed in 1977 (fig. 10). In it, they spent a day naked in a cage labeled "Homo Sapiens. Mammals. Male and Female." According to the Gerlovins, the cage symbolically protected them from "our motherland of vapid propaganda" and, as they later explained after leaving the Soviet Union, Western "monetarist hegemony" as well. Evidently, while in the cage, they were products to be looked at, but not to be bought or sold, or perhaps pure spirits not to be violated in their pristine, inviolate surroundings. In another piece from that year, *Costumes,* they were photographed wearing full-length gowns on which were drawn their body outlines, breasts, and genitalia.[3] Certainly, both pieces challenged Soviet prudery as well as the social conditioning and cultural expectations of the gender roles each was expected to play.

Tatiana Nazarenko and Natalia Nesterova were the two artists mentioned most often by younger women, both for the quality of their work and for the positions they held at the end of the Soviet period. In truth, neither would tell us exactly what they did in the artists' union, bygones being bygones, and the younger women were not entirely certain, either. Evidently, both served as jurors for various exhibitions, positions of power in that jurors not only had to select for quality, but also for appropriateness of subject matter, presumably in both local and international exhibitions. Short of going through union archival material, if it exists, we cannot

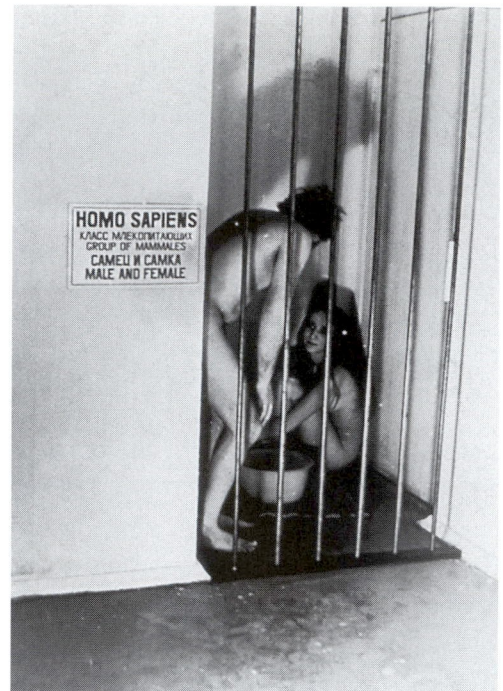

10. Valerii Gerlovin and Rimma Gerlovina, *Zoo, March 7, 1977,* 1977, gelatin silver print. (Courtesy Jane Voorhees Zimmerli Art Museum, Rutgers, The State University of New Jersey. The Norton and Nancy Dodge Collection of Nonconformist Art from the Soviet Union.)

speculate further what they did and whether they were held in awe, fear, or respect. But we know that their friends—their contemporaries—like and respect them. So we assume only the best about them.

Tatiana Nazarenko

Tatiana Nazarenko (b. 1944) lives in Moscow and paints in a realistic style (fig. 11). She graduated from the Surikov Art Institute in 1968. She is one of the few artists we met who include narrative elements, sometimes historical, in her work. This interview was given in 1995 and its main points were reiterated in meetings afterward.

RB: Have you ever felt discrimination?

TN: No. My last name is Nazarenko, which has a masculine ending. When I first began to exhibit—and some of my works were large in size—many people told me that they thought a powerful man made my work. They would say, "We are astonished that such a lovely young woman painted such works."

RB: And at school?

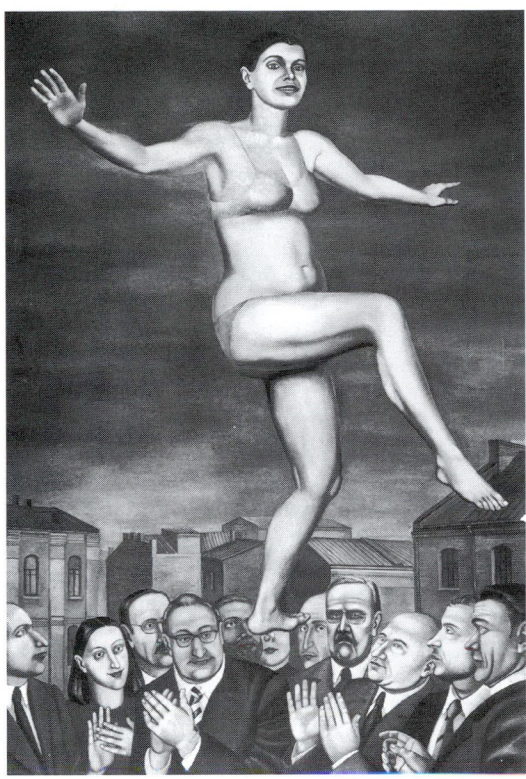

11. Tatiana Nazarenko, *Circus Actress*, 1984, oil on canvas. (Courtesy Tatiana Nazarenko.)

TN: I knew that for my graduation piece, I would have to present something safe and acceptable. So I painted a work about motherhood. I was very aware of what I did. There were some powerful women students then. We were rather uncomfortable with all the attention even after we started our careers. It was like, "Look at the girls!" We tried to show that we were no different from the men, especially since I was discouraged from studying in the monumental-painting department. All my life I have been stretching my own canvases and doing the necessary physical work. I never allowed anybody to help me. I carried heavy canvases and other art supplies. I did the hard work. My hand is as capable as any man's.

RB: Did this bother you very much?

TN: Not at all. I couldn't care less what people thought or think. The only time I felt an obstacle as a woman was when I was pregnant and gave birth while working on a large painting. At that moment, I was forced to decide between art or the child. Well, I chose art. That led to a divorce. I remarried and now have a second child. Physically now, things are a little bit more difficult than they were. But I have proved that I can be an artist and a woman. My divorce was due to difficult circumstances in that my studio was not where we lived. My grandmother, a strong, wonderful person who took care of me, said she would take of the baby if I moved in with her. My husband did not agree to that arrangement. And so the marriage ended. But there is something more. A man can devote himself entirely to his profession. He can stay overnight in his studio. I can't do that even though I have a shower and a hot-water heater in my studio. I am a woman and I use creams and lotions. So I prefer the comfort of my home.

RB: Were you in the union?

TN: Yes. Both Natalia Nesterova and I joined in 1969. It was the only way to exist. The union gave us studios, access to supplies, and commissions. For exhibitions, things were more difficult. Some works were accepted and others rejected. One work was removed three times from different exhibitions. Who knows why? First, the works were selected by a party committee from the union painting department. Then there was a higher party committee, then a selected jury. Then, there were two women who had a final say and made the final decisions. One time, a work of mine passed all the tests, but a call came down from somebody to remove a work just before the opening. The director had been told to remove it. But this was for political, not gender, reasons.

RB: How did you function in the union?

TN: I was in many different union offices, but I never felt discrimination as a woman, even though there were usually fewer works by women than by men in exhibitions. Perhaps it was tied to the fact that women are busier with family responsibilities. But I was always more like a boy. I always tried to run faster, not to lag behind.

RB: Did you ever participate in women's shows?

TN: Never.

RB: Was there equal opportunity at the institute?

TN: There were many women in the applied-arts departments. But no woman could occupy a position of power in any discipline.

RB: Tell me about *Circus Actress* [see fig. 11].

TN: Rumor had it that I had a successful career, but that is not entirely true. In 1982, I submitted several works for a show in Hamburg, but I was not allowed out of Russia to attend the opening. I was considered to be one of those who should not be permitted to go abroad. So I painted this picture as an assertion of my own freedom. All those officials standing below and clapping their hands are applauding my freedom, but in fact I am locked in, free in my art above the crowd, but not free in fact. I am like a tightrope walker who could fall at any moment. I settled the score with several people. In this picture, I painted all the officials who barred my trip and who barred me from other things. They said to my face that I was such a good artist and that they liked me enormously, but they really fooled me. You know, I held high positions and traveled all over the country even when I was in my twenties. I felt wonderful, powerful; and then it all changed. As the union began to ignore me, the underground artists began to respect me. That was good. I also want to say here, as embarrassing as it is for me to say so, but people said I either kissed somebody or slept with somebody to get someplace in the union, but I swear to you that I never had any type of sexual encounter with any officials.

RB: What about your male colleagues in the union?

TN: They were polite, but I am certain that they thought I did not advance only because of my art. Well, there was always gossip about me. I am used to it.

RB: Did you paint so-called feminine themes?

TN: Only my children, if you want to call that a feminine theme.

RB: What was it like at union meetings?

TN: Gender was not an issue, even if only men were at a meeting. More important was nationality—how many Russians, Ukrainians, or Jews in a show. On the other hand, if I signed my name "Tatiana Nazarenko," people would know I am a woman, but if I signed it "T. Nazarenko," they might not.

In 1988, Nazarenko used an image similar to *Circus Actress* in her *Circus in the Square.* In that work, a woman in bra and panties also performs on a tightrope far above a street in a neighborhood of low-slung buildings. And through the 1990s, she has painted what appears to be a series about the imagined life of Adam and Eve, or at least a naked couple, who live on a tabletop amid the bric-a-brac of objects and plants. She says that after perestroika she realized how small we all are, that we are like little ants, powerless. One of her more startling works, because it dates from 1970, is titled *Portrait of a Circus Actress* and shows an enormously large-scale woman who dominates the room because of her size, sitting cross-legged on a chair. She smokes a cigarette distractedly. In the far corner, away from her gaze, a much smaller man stands on his hands, staring at her imploringly. It is a moot point whether this is a statement about the artist's power or about the power structure. It is also not consistent with certain works she created during the 1980s in which a nude woman is surrounded by dressed men and women. Like virtually all other interviewees, she did not articulate a clear position on male-female relationships and, given the context of those earlier times, had probably not thought about it to any great extent then, either. Nevertheless, her works and the record of her professional career are important markers on the way to a more aggressive feminine presence in the 1990s, and, from what we understood, her significance is becoming increasingly recognized and appreciated.

Natalia Nestevora (b. 1944) also paints the human figure, but in more-fanciful ways (fig. 12). Years ago, she, too, selected works for union exhibitions, but denies that she served on juries. She also has little interest in feminist concerns, insisting that art is art regardless of the gender of its maker. Although a very pleasant person with whom we have spent several delightful evenings in Moscow and in New York, she is quite tough-minded about art. In her own words, she has said, "I never had a feeling about myself as a woman because I work at the same level as a man. I have had shows at the same level and in general have behaved as an equal, not as some girl or fair maiden. The word to describe me is *artist*. Call me by my

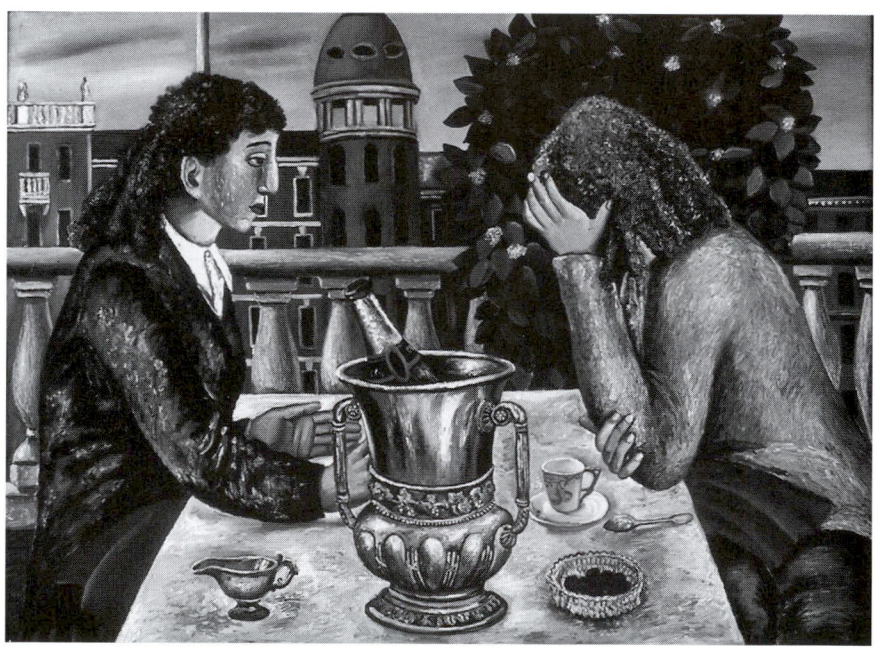

12.   Natalia Nesterova, *Talk,* 1982, oil on canvas. (Courtesy Jane Voorhees Zimmerli Art Museum, Rutgers, The State University of New Jersey. The Norton and Nancy Dodge Collection of Nonconformist Art from the Soviet Union. Copyright © Natalia Nesterova / Licensed by VAGA, New York.)

feminine noun or the masculine one. I don't care. I am an artist." Like others who projected great personal strength, Nestevora comes from a line of strong, supportive women. One of her grandmothers, widowed at a young age, was a doctor and a teacher. Her mother was an architect. Each took care of their families without the benefit of housekeepers. Known to younger artists, her no-nonsense approach, one imagines, has had an effect, however direct or indirect.

The New Generation

THE CONCERN for a feminist art and a feminist point of view during the 1990s did not move in a straight line. Contradictions abound. Some artists, angry about the roles they must play as both artist and homemaker, still resist any association with feminist thinking. Others see their situation as entirely normal. Some insist on change, but will try to bring it about as individuals, not as part of a collective force. The reasoning behind this position, we feel, is spectacularly flawed and is only just now beginning to be understood properly. Many feel that men get exhibitions on the basis of their strengths as artists, as individuals. For a woman to try to obtain them otherwise is tantamount to her admitting that she cannot achieve success on her own, that she is not as good as male artists. Feminist or all-women shows connote failure, according to this line of thought. So, forming professional alliances among women is ultimately a self-defeating proposition; networking implies acceptance of second-rate performance levels. What has been misunderstood and largely ignored, and is only just now being recognized, is that men have been informally networking all along, supporting one another, selecting one another's works for shows, limiting the number of exhibition slots for women, and discouraging women from becoming artists. Only a very rare woman can emerge victorious over that juggernaut. A mediocre male artist has a better chance at professional success than does a strong woman artist. Now, finally understanding the inequities of this kind of reasoning, younger artists have realized that in organization there is strength, and in organization there is, as a result, a turn to specific women's issues.

But this is still not universally understood or appreciated. We want to begin this section with Irina Bazileva's interview. She is a lawyer and respected art critic, an international traveler, who was probably not aware of the contradictions in her discussions of various aspects of the contemporary scene. But this was typical and totally understandable, since artists and critics are still grappling, and will probably always grapple, with the way they were instructed to think before the fall of Communism and with the unimagined ways they are able to do so now. As a participant in several feminist conferences in Moscow and abroad, she is well aware of current ideas, but her attitudes particularly about the presentation of the body reflect a conservative Soviet ethos still strong in Russia. She also indicated, albeit indirectly, a strong sense of Russian nationalism vis-à-vis the inevitable penetration of her country by western cultural values. This interview was given in 1998.

Irina Bazileva

RB: How do you read the current scene?

IB: Socially, men had more trouble than women, especially during Soviet times and even during perestroika. They could not earn much money and become really involved in self-expression. They felt humiliated. Women had it easier. They were more flexible, even though they worked hard and also ran the household. Through the seventy years of Communist rule, women were able to keep a better sense of their self-esteem. They have no need of self-reproach.

RB: What about relationships?

IB: In the earlier days, relationships between men and women were more like partnerships than like competitions. In the art world, the situation was much the same, especially among dissident artists. There was no difference in the social borders between men and women. The artists could be free within their dissident world. But now, a generational difference exists. Some of the younger women artists have taken up feminism. There really is no basis for it in Russian history. It is a Western import. Now, younger women artists want to make gender-derived statements based on Western art, especially when they show abroad. They will use gimmicks to that effect, or allow things to be said about them that are not necessarily true, as long as they get some attention. So women have become more distinct and different from men in their art, and will not necessarily follow their true inclinations. Now women are free to express anything, which is OK. There are no rules of correctness anymore.

RB: What about images of women?

IB: Going back in Russian history to the period even before the Revolution, we can say that artists never considered women as sex objects. Rather, they chose to paint women for their beauty and individuality. There might have been something erotic in their approach, but they saw a woman as a beautiful person, perhaps with some spiritual power, but not as a sex object. Then commercial advertisements were introduced from the West in which women were regarded as sex objects. This kind of imagery is not indigenous to us.

RB: Are there feminist organizations?

IB: Yes. They are mostly political. They get most of their money from the West and are basically make-work organizations that hold conferences and publish reports. Women artists want to be individuals and don't want to join any groups. Let us say, for example, that Artist A has nothing in common with Artist B and so she does not want to join a group with Artist B. She wants to keep her separate identity. She probably also wants to keep her freedom, in part based on her memory of totalitarian times and what went on in organizations in the past.

Natalia Kamenetskaia

Natalia Kamenetskaia (b. early 1960s) is at the center of feminist activity in Moscow. An artist in her own right, she teaches at the Russian State University for the Humanities in Moscow and has organized conferences that have explored gender issues in Russia. In 1989, she helped form Idioma in 1989, a research-oriented group. She was instrumental in seeing through to publication the issue of a dual-language edition of *Heresies* in 1992 concerned with women's issues in Russia (see n. 2 in the Introduction). We have spoken with her several times both in Russia and in New York. The following is based on an interview given in 1995.

NK: In 1990, I curated a few experimental shows as a result of my interest in issues concerning women artists.

RB: What is the situation for women, what interests them, and what are they preoccupied with?

NK: Right now, women are not very aware of their situation. That is, where there is money, there is awareness, and we have no money. There are women's political organizations, but artists do not belong to them. Many of the women involved are politicians, and they often have financially successful husbands who are also occupied with politics. They are really not interested in our concerns, and have no interest in raising funds for us.

RB: What about the conferences you have held?

NK: They were mostly about cultural paradigms in different areas such as philosophy, literary criticism, and ethnography. They generated a lot of interest about gender and feminist issues. Recently, I took part in a colloquium with Swedish women who wrote and edited a feminist magazine. They were not artists. Our representatives were women artists who were not feminists. The match-up did not work very well. There is, however, some interest in gender issues now, particularly about male cross-dressing. They don't use homosexuality as a theme, just the cross-dressing. Vladik Ivanishev, for example, plays Marilyn Monroe, and also dresses up as Hitler and Saint Sebastian. He shows up places in outrageous costumes, but there is no movement to speak of.

RB: Have you found anything like a female style or set of themes?

NK: Earlier, I thought there were such things, but now nobody knows. Earlier, we acknowledged traditional women's art as being craft oriented.

RB: We have met artist couples, and invariably they say that the husband is the main creator, the idea person.

NK: Yes, generally speaking, it is thought here that men are more talented. Of course it is not true, but men would like to think so. In my experience, we have a greater number of talented women—at least here in Moscow. But things will change. For example, the Center for Contemporary Art would never have invited me earlier to take part in an event, but I was recently involved in one. On the other hand, there is a strong conservative mood as well. Many women want to return to older ideals, to stay home, to be taken care of. That is, they want more patriarchy, an emphasis on traditional roles for women such as doing the laundry, bearing children, et cetera.

RB: How do women react to all of this?

NK: In the early 1990s, when we started out, there was a lot of enthusiasm. Now we're worn out. We're tired of life, of struggling. Oddly, artist couples seem to fare better. Maybe it takes two to succeed.

RB: With the lessening of moral strictures, is there much in the way of body art?

NK: There are some performances. The artists undress, perform some kind of action or show photographs of themselves. It is a new kind of hype. One recent performance had an artist leading another artist, naked, on a chain. But we do not have really graphic events concerning, say, birth or menstruation, such as you have in the States. It was tried here, but prohibited by gallery sponsors. Nudity is not so popular here. In and of itself it is too primitive an activity to resolve cultural problems.

RB: What about support groups?

NK: We don't have any. The problem is an economic one. It is very difficult for galleries to survive, so they must sell what makes money for them. They are, for the most part, not interested in experimental art. So support groups can't help with sales. There are no organizations of women artists. A while ago, there was an organization called the Union of Women Cinematographers, but I don't know if it still exists. I have contacts with support groups in other countries, and we do try to plan joint ventures—publications, conferences—but it's difficult.

Kamenetskaia recently (in 2000) told us that an overall change has taken place in feminist agitation in Russia. Initially, she and others, including those in other fields, stressed gender issues at the expense of feminist concerns. She finds now a greater response to the latter, especially those concerned with birthing and the primitive hospital care women receive (see interview with Ludmila Gorlova). Her idea is that before fundamental changes can be made in modifying the cultural constructions of gender, both men and women must become more sensitive to the particular concerns of women. This extends beyond fundamental biological needs to those concerned with the marketplace such as finding more outlets in the art market for women artists and explorations of subject matter generated by women about women's thoughts, fantasies, and visions. She and others hope that ultimately traditional stereotypes of women will disappear as the particular needs of women are addressed and greater parity is achieved in public life. This, of course, is a very long-term project.

Anna Alchuk

Kamenetskaia is obviously in touch with women artists who are comfortable with feminist concerns. Their attitudes toward a feminist agenda and to a feminist subject matter is at variance with those of other artists, as will be borne out in the following interviews. Through Kamenetskaia, we met and spoke with artist-photographer Tania Antoshina (b. early 1960s) on several occasions. At a dinner with Kamenetskaia in Antoshina's apartment in 1998 we were introduced to photographer and critic Anna Alchuk (b. early 1960s). Antoshina's husband, the model for many of her photographs (see fig. 13), prepared and served dinner. This was quite surprising, since most Russian men, in our experience, do not share many, or any, domestic responsibilities with their spouses. We turned on the tape recorder early in the evening and left it on until we left. We include the interview with Alchuk first, and then the interview with Antoshina.

RB: When did you begin to participate in exhibitions?

AA: In 1990. My first show was called *The Woman Worker*. It was a conceptual exhibition by Moscow women artists. This was our first attempt to put on a feminist show. Each artist presented her works—for example, Irina Nakhova did an installation; Vera Khlebnikova showed collages. Since then, I have participated in group and solo exhibitions. One of my pieces in *The Woman Worker* represented a stove pasted over with pink paper to symbolize a womb. Near it were sprouting crystal mushrooms that could be interpreted as phalluses. I also had some photographs in the show. What interests me is the discourse that surrounds all my work. One work, called *Three Times Three*, is pure appropriation. I took a photo of a bas-relief by Motovilova at the Elektrozavodskaya Metro Station. I was struck by the regularity of each panel in the relief. There are three women and one man in the center. The women are tenderly holding to their bosoms the shafts of cannons. There are also propeller blades, all of which are types of phalluses. I was astonished to make this discovery. At the Krasnopresnenskaya Metro Station, I discovered three aggressive kulaks holding hammers, signifying the quintessence of phallic power in the Soviet Union. These images were part of a project I started, to find images of women at metro stations. I found many such sexual images that represented to me metaphors for the motherland.

RB: Did you study art?

AA: No. I wrote poetry and still do so. Then I began to make photographs; I don't paint at all. Let me show you another photo that was in the same show. It is based on a Stalinist poster dedicated to the Exposition of Agricultural Farming. Stalin is in the background of the arch, under which we see a huge mass of people celebrating. They seem as if in a madhouse. I enlarged the faces of a woman and a man. They look absolutely degenerate, out of their minds. For another exhibition, this one in St. Petersburg in 1994 at Gallery 21, I photographed six men in the pose of the Venus de Milo [see fig. 4]. They are headless. All six are well known in the Moscow art world—critics, writers, artists, including Sergei Epikhin, Andrei Kovalev, and Oleg Kulik. They were happy to pose for me. I intended to reverse the usual order of the male gaze observing an ideal female body. It is no accident that the Venus de Milo has no arms. She cannot protect herself from voyeurism. Neither can these men. I also did another photo for an exhibition in 1997 with Tania Antoshina, Masha Chuikova, Nina Kotyel, and Elena Elagina, a variation on the Venus de Milo theme. This one simply had headless male bodies lined up in a row. The viewer can make detailed comparisons. The work turned out to be very funny, since people tried to identify the subjects.

RB: What is your occupation?

AA: I worked for a time as an editor, then I did freelance writing. I made an easy transfer to visual materials with my husband when we began to do performances in 1989. We came under the influence of the conceptual group Collective Actions, and worked with people like Igor Makarevich and Elena Elagina [see interview]. It was then that I began to photograph men famous in the art world. A few years later I asked some to pose absolutely naked. They were not used to this kind of request, but they were very happy to pose for me. My conditions were that they had to be naked. They could acquire some object that would function as a phallic symbol—a knife, a sword. I was interested in how they would react to the photographs. This was part of a project I called *Figures of Law* for which the men took off their clothes. A few even seemed to do so with pleasure. They accepted it as a game and did not feel offended that a woman was photographing them. It all went smoothly. It was done in the apartment of Nina Kotyel and one of the men was her husband. [When we interviewed Kotyel, he constantly interrupted and insisted on speaking for her.] They all behaved with ease. I don't think that American men of the same stature would have behaved in the same way. And I don't think I would have been able to find too many Russian women authors willing to pose for me.

RB: What prompted you to explore this subject matter?

AA: I lived in America for a year, and I think I was influenced by American feminism. I found it very interesting to figure out how American feminism can be applied effectively to our experiences. So I began to explore Russian phallocentrism.

RB: Let's get back to Russian women authors.

AA: You have to understand that our situation is different from yours. Our men, I believe, are not as phallocentric as American men. Let me explain by telling you about another project of mine. This one, in reaction to American feminism, was called *Double Play*. In it, I am both the subject and the object. I was the one photographed. Another man and I, a very handsome man, wanted to be photographed in women's clothing. In thirty-four photographs, laid out in pairs, we are dressed and posed exactly alike, the sequence going from a maximal feminine appearance to a maximal masculine one. The sense of masculinity grew as the sequence progressed. People commented that in the earlier photographs, the man looked more feminine than I did, that he was playing at being a woman. In some photos, I might have looked more masculine, depending on the clothing worn and the way makeup was applied.

Also, we re-enacted certain billboard advertisements as well as some pornographic images of the New Russians [the newly rich]. I was interested in the way images of femininity and masculinity were framed and constructed.

RB: The genders cross in this project.

AA: They do. What it is saying is that our education is artificial—the way we dress and the way we are raised is totally artificial. What we are biologically and what we are socially are different. Thinking about such matters is still new for us. Simone de Beauvoir's *The Second Sex* was just published in Russia. Can you believe it? I have to tell you something. I just read about Olga Shapir, a nineteenth-century writer, in the feminist magazine *Vestnik*. She was a revelation to me. I had no idea that we had such a powerful feminist in Russia. We have to find out more about our past.

Alchuk also suggested that in post-Soviet Russia, an interest in erotic subject matter did not necessarily mean an interest in pornography. Instead, such an interest could reflect and, after the collapse of the Soviet system, finally allow an individual to express his or her relation to the chosen subject rather than to one's relation being subsumed within a collective narration. (Imagine a painting of a bathhouse in which several nude workers are seen showering after a hard day's work on the collective farm rather than a study of a single worker at his or her toilette.) In effect, artists during the Soviet period had to substitute group images for more personal concerns, expressions, and modes of inquiry that could include how individual subjects might react in specific situations.[1] It is also important to keep in mind that the artist's gaze, whether male or female, might be more concerned with, at least in the first years of the new democratic government, exploring aspects of personal freedom than with libidinous urges.

In regard to the images of women in the metro stations, which were created in the 1940s, Alchuk wrote an important article in 1998 further exploring their meanings. She found that several had expressions of rage in war scenes and that they projected enormous energy, especially in scenes of labor in which the women drove tractors and worked as farm laborers. Alchuk noted that gender differences were eradicated. The women are shown working hard; their muscles bulge. They are presented as the ideal image of a collective-farm worker in that their bodies, lacking individualized characteristics, are desexualized and belong to the collective. Erotic pleasure, such as it might appear, is sublimated into images of energetic movement, all in the name of collective production for the state.[2]

Tania Antoshina

This interview took place on the same evening as the one with Alchuk. Antoshina showed us several photographs of her husband and some of their male friends in nude poses based on canonical examples of modern art—by Manet, Gauguin, Picasso, and others—in which the subject in the original includes one or more women. We illustrate here Antoshina's version of Manet's *Olympia* (fig. 13).

RB: What about this photograph?

TA: I did it in 1997. I would say that all traditional and contemporary art could be called one vast male museum or a museum for men, because museums were constituted to represent the desires of men or male ambitions. This is clear because most painters of masterpieces are male. Yet now we have many women artists, but the situation has not changed appreciably. I want to create a women's museum simply as a

13. Tania Antoshina, *Olympia*, 1997, photograph. (Courtesy Tania Antoshina.)

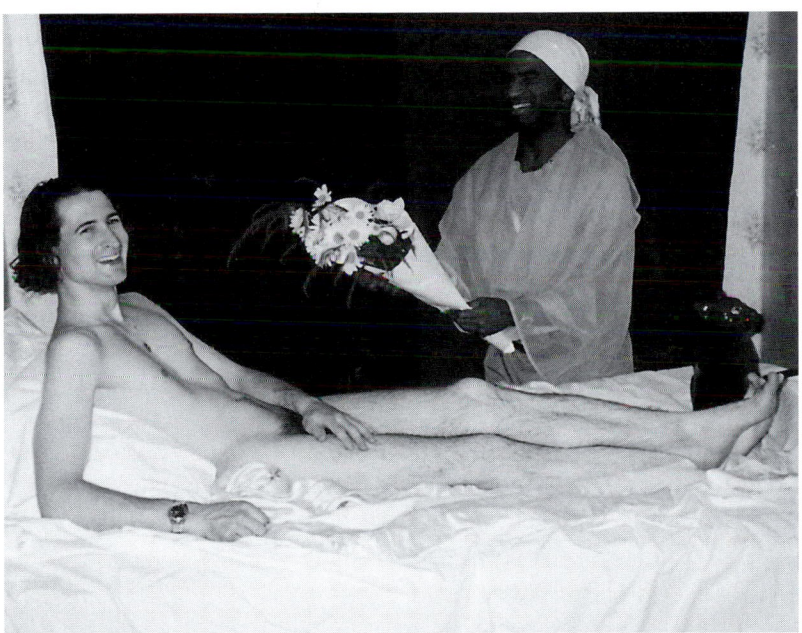

gesture, not with the intention of making constant changes, but so that what I am about as a woman and what my work is about is understood. In 1997, I had two shows at Marat Gellman's gallery; the first one was with photographer Tania Liberman [see interview] and performance artist Alena Martinova [see interview]. The title was *Russian Women.* The second one was called *Women's Museum.* Journalists wanted to know if such a museum exists. I gave odd answers and finally I lost control. I told them that, yes, such a museum did exist—in my home. It would be a place for young, talented women to show their work, particularly women interested in gender issues. I told them that this is good for Russia, and a new and interesting development in contemporary art. Then soon after Natasha Kamenetskaia and I went to a consortium of women's organizations. They asked what I was doing. I told them I was creating a women's museum. They wanted to help, saying that they supported all kinds of women's initiatives. They provided information about where to apply for grants. So maybe something might come of it. But maybe not. The consortium is not really interested in culture or art, but rather in social problems, and we are not very good at filling out applications—at least I am not.

RB: What you want, what might have started as a joke, is very important. When I spoke with Aidan Salakhova and Lena Kuprina [both run a gallery; their interview follows], they said that Russian women skipped a beat in their evolution as artists. They said that women had equality and even drove tanks. So now women wanted to be more feminine than militant, that they did not want to be militant in the way that American feminists are militant.

TA: Since you mention Aidan's name, I want to say, apropos her interest in androgyny and equality, that in the Soviet state, all kinds of individual characteristics and sexual particularities were more or less officially neutralized or nullified. Differences in male and female psychologies were not considered, nor was it customary to discuss sex or one's sex life. We had become androgynous. We were all the same. We were people, ciphers, void of individual potentialities and particularities, including differences based on one's sex. I remember a telecast in which a Russian woman declared that in Russia there is no sex. This was a characteristic statement—we don't have sexual activities because we have no gender differences. There is no masculine or feminine. We are all equal. Many people believed this, they sincerely believed this, and experienced themselves this way.

RB: I've seen posters of women represented as mother-heroes or as tank drivers deprived of their femininity, of their sexuality. But men are not deprived of their manliness.

TA: Yes, they were all supposed to be alike. Women were not embarrassed to have male characteristics. But I have to say that Russian men were also deprived of certain male aspects because of the emphases on virtue, bravery, and honor.

RB: Then you are saying that an interest in androgyny today is in some way a continuation of the Soviet de-emphasis on sexual difference and the corresponding emphasis on similarity.

TA: Something like that.

Natasha Kamenetskaia joined the conversation at this point.

RB: Natasha, what do you think?

NK: I have a different view. We always had a double consciousness here. In Soviet times, we had kitchen-table conversations that were always about sex. That's all anybody had on their minds. Recently, one lady from a foreign country complained to me that all the prostitutes in her country come from Russia. Where did they come from if we did not have prostitution? But it was not proper to speak of such matters in Soviet times. Officially, there were no prostitutes. My point is that we cannot rely on or believe what was officially stated. At least the intelligentsia knew the difference.

TA: The mass of people did not know what was going on. What is there to talk about when you don't know what's going on? In the countryside, people really did not listen to ideological talk or know what the intelligentsia thought. I lived in Siberia, not Moscow, which is like a separate state. I came into contact with all kinds of people, simple people. We didn't sit around the kitchen table discussing sex. We chatted, maybe said something angry about the state or something about politics, but we never discussed sex.

The conversation faltered at this point, with Kamenetskaia and Antoshina clearly rehearsing an argument they had had many times before. But the interesting point that emerged here was the suggestion that Soviet gender policies in some way contributed to the interest in androgyny in Russia today, but with the clear difference that the Soviets wanted everybody to think they were socially equal, whereas contemporary artists look at androgyny as an interesting biological and gender issue that compels one to look at traditional gender constructions in new ways.

Aidan Salakhova

Salakhova (b. 1964) is an artist and, with Lena Kuprina, a gallery owner. Although a powerful artist and personality in her own right, and one who experienced directly the economic ups and downs of the post-Soviet period, she has had easier access to the art world than many others because her father, Tair Taimurovich Salakhov (b. 1928), was first secretary of the USSR Artists' Union. She was interviewed twice, once by telephone from New York in 1996 and again in Moscow in 1998. In her remarks she extends the discussion we had with Kamenetskaia and Antoshina, but she also describes her training and her life as a woman in post-Soviet Russia.

RB: Tell me about your art training.

AS: I studied in art school from the eighth through the eleventh grades, and then at the Surikov Art Institute from 1982 to 1987. I was always interested in painting, but originally I wanted to study biology and genetics. My entire family are artists, so I began to draw as a child. My father always made regulations, which now I think were good ones. One needed to have a career, but since he was from the East, from Baku, he encouraged me to marry at the age of eighteen, as many women do. Actually, he raised me to have a career, make something of myself, and then get married and have children, and somehow combine family and work. He was different from other eastern men in that he presented me with possibilities. And for that I am very grateful.

RB: Do you have siblings?

AS: A sister, a wonderful artist who married at eighteen and became a housewife.

RB: What was art school like?

AS: My situation was very complicated, because my father was and still is a very famous cultural power. You can imagine that my successes were attributed to him, as if he did my work for me, as if I had no talent of my own. This has been difficult for me. But I had no problems in art school. It was one of the first democratic schools in that we did not have to wear uniforms. Also, there were the same number of boys as girls.

RB: And your teachers?

AS: Men for the most part, particularly the art teachers. The academic subjects were taught by women. There were very few women art teachers.

RB: Was there much competition between boys and girls?

AS: I didn't experience any. But I have my own theory. I think that an artist is a bisexual being, and one cannot judge from a painting if the artist is male or female. A male artist is as feminine as a woman artist and vice versa. Their characteristics are equalized.

RB: Did your teachers have equal hopes for your success as they did for the boys?

AS: In principle, yes. And right after graduation, when perestroika began, there were some democratic exhibitions. For a youth exhibition, I submitted a picture titled *Steel Orgasm against an Orange Background,* and the jury took it.

RB: Were you treated as an equal with men?

AS: Yes, in my career, but not in my home life. My husband was a painter and he was very jealous of the fact that I, too, was involved with creative matters. His position was that women had no place in the art world. At one point, my pictures were selling better and at higher prices than his, and then, as a well-known gallery owner, I sold his paintings. He was envious and jealous, to the point that he said that if we were to live together I would have to quit painting. I did so for four years. I know this kind of thing happens to many young women. You make something of yourself, then the problems begin in your private life, especially if the man is not ready to have an equal relationship. Russian men have an image of a woman as a wife, a mother, one who stands all day in the kitchen making soup. This is a very strong ingrained image in most men's minds. So problems arise. During the four years I did not paint, I had a lot of mental anguish and I was depressed. Then I got divorced and stopped being depressed. In truth, I never stopped being involved in art, and this didn't help matters. When I gave birth, I realized that a child needs both a happy mother and a self-realized person. That helped me resolve my personal problem. Having a child gave me strength. In general, our young women do not fully understand the importance of self-realization.

RB: Are there any organizations in Moscow that lend support to women?

AS: I don't know of any. When I get together with friends, we talk about problems of self-realization in our private lives. We don't discuss social issues. I have girlfriends like Lena, who is an art critic and a curator and a partner in the gallery. We all have similar problems, but we are very strong. We work and make our own living. Men could not accept our new position.

RB: It is interesting that your sense of your new consciousness emerged without support groups.

AS: You have to consider what happened after perestroika. There were rapid changes in our lives, and the men took these changes very hard.

Women quickly adapted to the new situation and began to act accordingly, while the men lagged behind. A woman is used to adjusting or adapting to different circumstances. We had to be crafty and learn how to buy meat without standing in line. Women had to make quick decisions in everyday life. These complications prepared us for coping with the present difficulties. We immediately understood that we needed to act. But our men felt left behind in the new capitalist economy. They still clung to old conditions, and somehow could not work through their problems. At that point, women got ahead of them.

RB: What are present-day relationships between men and women artists?

AS: I currently have a male friend, an artist, with whom I have a very good and equal relationship. Of course, this depends on the woman and the conditions she establishes. I was weak and insecure with my first husband. Society said that I should be docile. I didn't believe it, but when you live with a person whom you love, and your husband holds such beliefs, then you begin to think that perhaps you are wrong, that you are have illusions about yourself. So when he demanded that I stop painting for four years, I thought it was wrong, but I more or less agreed.

RB: How did your father react?

AS: He was very upset, and when I got divorced, he was very supportive. Actually, it was I who earned the living in the family. I was the one who fed the family. When I quit painting, we had no money, and problems began. He had suffered because I had earned more money. He felt that we should be able to live on the little that he made. I turned down three exhibitions, and I had a list of clients who wanted my pictures, but I gave it all up. I suffered enormously and had to see an analyst. That helped me get back on my feet.

RB: I want to ask you about your art, about your pictures of hermaphrodites.

AS: I am very interested in the hermaphroditic image precisely because it is both male and female. I always paint women [fig. 14]. My model is a former bodybuilder, and I show how women in our time assume male characteristics. I feel that if we accept the fact that men have female characteristics, the same goes for women. It is a sort of bisexuality. If we accept this, then perhaps we can understand one another much better. The problem is that men will not accept their female sides.

RB: Why don't you represent male genitalia?

AS: My focus is more on the feminine aspect. I am also working on a video in which we will see an image of a woman as she was before assuming male features and then one after. I don't really have in mind

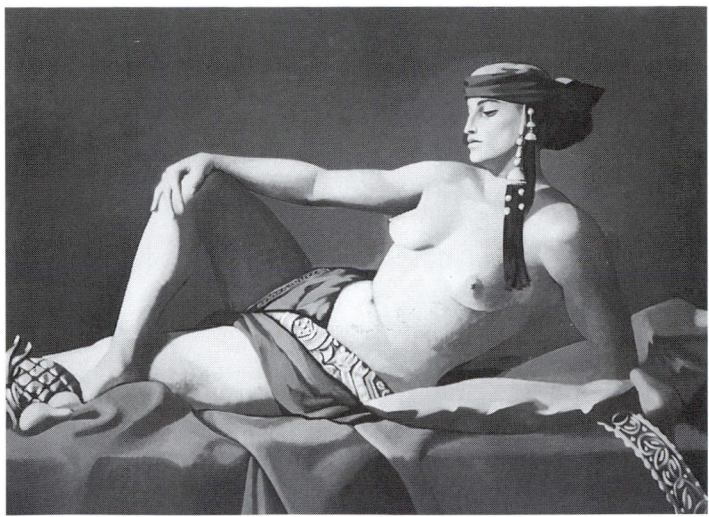

14. Aidan Salakhova, *Nude,* 1998, oil on canvas. (Courtesy Aidan Salakhova.)

actual physical attributes, but images that appeal to the imagination. So the women I paint are anatomically women, not true hermaphrodites. There are no male genitalia.

RB: Should your images be imitated by real women? Are your images to be used as models for women in the future?

AS: I am only speaking of acceptance within one's own self, that we share both male and female features. This will help equalize our differences. Perhaps we will be better able to appreciate one another as people rather than keep the division between male and female personalities.

RB: Do you aim for obliteration of borderlines?

AS: Yes, but as a mindset. If we keep the division, we are divided inwardly. Of course I mean psychologically, not physiologically.

RB: Have you noticed any changes in art during the past few years? Are there changes especially in women's work?

AS: I don't want to separate art into male and female. I don't consider it correct. For me, there is no division. I want to eliminate such categories.

At this moment, Lena Kuprina joined the conversation.

RB: You mentioned that women are more adaptable, more flexible, than men.

AS: A woman's psyche *is* more flexible. Lena is the one in her family who has earned money.

LK: My husband was depressed for four years.

AS: He is an artist and could not go to work in advertising where he could make some money. He wanted to sell his paintings, but nothing was happening. Lena and I worked at anything we could do to earn a living.

LK: You can't believe what we did. I have a child at home, a husband, and a mother-in-law who gets a very small pension. I will say that the psychological mood in the apartment depends on how much food is on the table. We also have other problems. I have to go to work and swallow my pride. I don't refuse to do such and such.

AS: All of our men have or had a similar attitude or position. My husband would say, "How can I do that?" We lived for one year in America, and I would ask him to find a job. I couldn't work because of the baby. He would answer, "I am an artist and I will be busy with my art. I am working. I am painting pictures." And I would tell him that nobody wants them. He would repeat that he is an artist and then ask if he should get a job unloading boxes at a supermarket. I would tell him I would do it if I had to.

LK: My husband would ask, "Why do you want to stop me from being an artist?" I didn't get divorced, and we still live together. I fell into a deep depression, but I continued working. Then I noticed that he was actually trying to do something, but somehow he could not manage to find a job, although he is a very talented designer. Very quietly, I began to push him to seek psychiatric help. It took an entire year. This is how I had to work on him—from underground, quietly.

AS: Lena's husband is a hero in our circle. He went, and it helped. Immediately, he found a job.

LK: Of course, he makes less money than I do, but basically he earns enough. When he began to work, his sense of creativity returned with his self-esteem.

AS: During the 1980s, our men thought that everything would remain as before.

LK: I would say that we all fell into a depression in the 1990s. In the late 1980s, our artists did well financially, but we went through a difficult time in 1991 and 1992.

AS: For four years, our male artists did not make any money. But to take a job meant courting a psychological breakdown.

LK: We tried to reason with them. We asked what there was to be upset about. Nobody was asking them to be janitors or wash floors. After all, in the West, artists are happy if they can find a job in advertising. Our men thought that such work was humiliating.

AS: They saw everything as a humiliation. "I am an artist and you are preventing me from doing my art," or so the litany went. "You expect me to empty garbage for you?" We did not then have a gallery. Contemporary works did not sell, so we began to working at an alternative market selling old paintings from the early twentieth century.

LK: For two months I did that. Things were very bad, so the manager suggested I sell at the market or in a bazaar. So the manager and I—not my husband—stood at the marketplace for about two months. The temperature was below zero. We stood from 5 A.M. on and traded stuff. We traded all sorts of things—clothing, whatever.

AS: When I returned from America, I had no gallery, no money for food, a small child. My husband remained in the States. So I began to sell Indian dresses. I stood outdoors with the baby in a carriage—three dollars a dress. I am now the owner of a well-known gallery and I am also a well-known artist. Men just couldn't hack it.

LK: Now, everything is going well. [This was just prior to the 1998 economic meltdown.] Male artists submit paintings. We are in a position to be choosy and to organize exhibitions that we like. Our clients for contemporary art are those who also buy old art. Aidan has a true gift of persuasion.

AS: At one time we had a debt of seventy thousand dollars. Any normal businessman would have closed the place. But we've paid our debts. We did it on our own.

LK: There are no sponsors for what we do. Banks will not give credit. The George Soros Foundation has been helpful, but basically, we run things with our own money. We depend on ourselves and nobody else.

AS: During the Soviet period, we all developed a dependency on the state. That has had a very negative psychological effect on all of us.

LK: If we did not get well paid, we blamed the state. Whatever problems we had, we blamed the state. The state became an excuse for everything. It crippled us. Now, if you want to make something of yourself, you have to rely on your own resources.

RB: Some of the older women I've spoken with say that there was equality during the Soviet years.

AS: There was no equality in family life. It was never so. Professionally, there was equality. I never felt oppressed professionally.

LK: On the other hand, I wanted to enter the international school of journalism after college. I found out that girls were not admitted. There was no explanation. They would tell me not to waste my time, that a woman would not be accepted. Nor could I have studied government policy for the same reason. A woman could study philology or literature or something about other nationalities. Or medicine.

AS: My mother used to warn me not to get into a foreign car because I would be followed. We were not permitted to socialize with foreigners. I recall in 1988, a bunch of foreigners arrived in Moscow for a special program. When I saw them I realized that I had an entirely different image of them. There was no correspondence to any reality. Foreign language instruction in school was so poor—rote and repetition—that we could not speak with them, anyway. This was done on purpose.

RB: Do you believe that women are stronger than men?

AS: Yes. At home, boys and girls were treated differently. A man was supposed to be strong even if he was weak. There are times when we are all strong or weak. I think things are changing now, even though it is still hard for a man to admit to a weakness.

Salakhova's comments about male weakness were not surprising after our hearing similar observations from several women. Somehow, between the actions of the Soviet government, the uncertainties of the new economy, and their femininization by women grade-school teachers, Russian men were programmed for weakness. But at the same time, virtually all interviewees complained about male domination. Even with some serious questioning, we could not discover to what extent the various comments were a form of necessary, self-aggrandizing posturing; whether the war between the sexes was out in the open; whether men knew what women thought about them and whether they cared; and, despite their comments, how weak and divided the women were, tolerating conditions they all agreed were horrible. Several expressed great anger with present and former husbands, but the kind of consciousness-raising that such anger engendered in the United States during the 1970s has yet to occur in the countries we visited.

Bela Matveeva

Salakhova's paintings are neoclassical in style with amply proportioned and idealized figures. In St Petersburg, we interviewed only one other artist, Bela Matveeva (b. 1961), whose works reflected an interest in androgyny. But her subjects evoke fin de siècle decadence and eroticism rather than Salakhova's sturdy brand of neoclassicism (fig. 15). Matveeva,

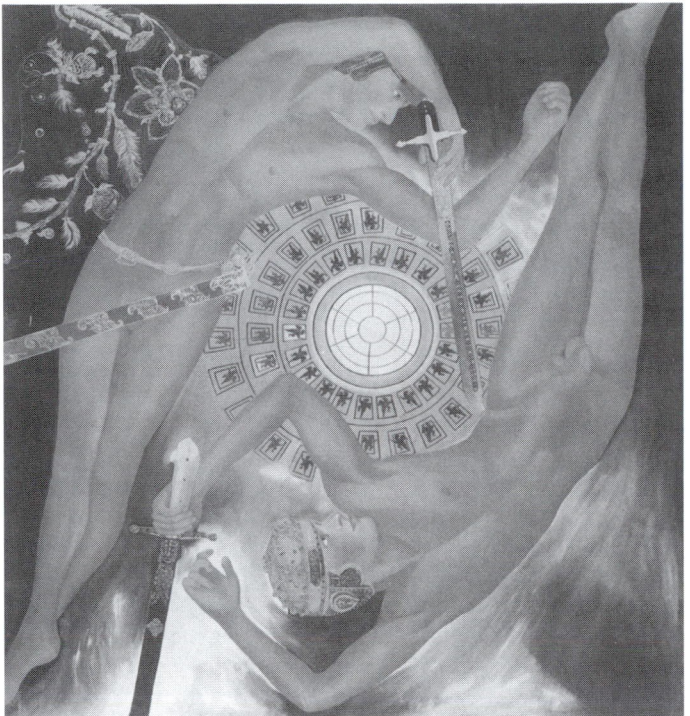

15. Bela Matveeva, *Roulette,* c. 1990, oil on canvas. (Courtesy Bela Matveeva.)

....

perhaps in keeping with the delicate style in which she works, revealed little hostility to men or to anybody or anything else. In fact, she created an aura of mystery about herself, also not unlike the figures she chooses to paint, constantly deflecting questions with subtle evasions and challenges. We interviewed her in 1995 and again in 1998.

BM: I was born in the southern Urals and came to study in St. Petersburg in 1979. I studied restoration techniques at the Serov School. I worked at restoring icons, as a window designer and a clothing designer.
RB: Did you feel any discrimination at school?
BM: I don't think so. Standards were the same, but perhaps the teachers, who wanted their students to become famous and therefore to bring glory to them, relied more on the boys. I can't really tell. I finished school in 1982.

RB: Who encouraged your ambition?

BM: It is an inner condition. Now, I have friends, but I seem to change them every few years. I have many male friends. Even though I have a daughter [born in 1983], I cannot identify with housewives.

RB: What about discrimination as an adult?

BM: I am actually glad when in certain situations I am treated as a woman. It is very pleasant. Allowances are made for me. Perhaps I play a game, which means I put myself on an equal level with men. I don't separate life from art. Art is a way in which I can reveal myself. As I constantly improvise in life, so I do the same in art. I can wear all kinds of masks—of a man, a woman, a bird, an animal. It is impossible for one to reveal oneself utterly. It is too dangerous. As for my work, I could never have shown my paintings during Soviet times.

RB: What about your inner voice?

BM: I am a woman and a mother. But there are several occasions where gender does not apply.

RB: What do you have in mind when you paint?

BM: It's too complicated to say, but I would have to say that there is something inside of me, something like an impulse. My pictures do not reflect life as it is. I do not paint in a realistic mode.

RB: There is an erotic quality in your work.

BM: Could be, but I hardly notice it.

RB: Do you find there is a women's issue?

BM: I don't feel any discrimination as a woman. But these are difficult times for everybody to exist independently. Sometimes something happens when an exhibition is being organized, but I don't connect it to my gender. It's true that men are unable to understand women and their desire for independence. There is the big war between the sexes, but one has to have a distance from it and remain philosophical. If there is discrimination here, it is with people from the Caucasus. With men, it is sort of a balancing act. There's no question that women feel weaker in certain situations. But we also have responsibilities—for the children. Men do not possess such instincts. They are not concerned with their children in the same way.

RB: Are there organizations in St. Petersburg concerned with women's issues?

BM: There are some, but I have no connection with them. They have no money. They are primarily social institutions and are themselves in need of money.

Alena Romanova

Alena Romanova (b. 1949) is a figure painter and a craftsperson who makes jewelry. She is also very much concerned with the female body, but not in the same way as Salakhova. In her interview, she revealed the exasperation many feel about living in Russia and also, more important from our point of view, that she had made a series of feminist paintings without realizing what she had done and without calling them by that name. Like virtually all the other interviewees, she sees herself as a strong, self-reliant, and highly motivated woman, but not always pleased or comfortable with being one. This interview dates from 1998.

RB: What about feminist issues in Russia?

AR: This is not a concern in the world in which we live. The roof over our heads is caving in on everybody. When you live in a catastrophic situation, male-female issues are not something to worry about. This is a problem for a calm, stable society. Anyway, our society is archaic, backward. We live in archaic space and time. Nothing has changed except that maybe Russia is finally trying to step over the threshold into civilization. We don't live in a civilized society; we are still like a clan, a family. This is a country of peasants.

RB: How does this affect you?

AR: Unconsciously, I don't know. Consciously, I am not comfortable. I am not a peasant, but a city person oriented toward European values. I don't fit in here, but nobody cares. I would have preferred to have been born in England.

RB: Where did you go to school?

AR: I went to the Polygraphic Institute. The Surikov Art Institute was too conservative. I could be myself at the Polygraphic. Elsewhere, it was a dictatorship.

RB: How was the school?

AR: There were more girls. No discrimination, but it is true that the teachers thought that the girls would eventually get married, have children, and drop their careers. Even so, the girls stood out more than the boys, who were not as serious as we were. I must admit, though, that about two-thirds of the girls did drop out. My parents were scientists and didn't want me to become an artist because they thought that artists were braggarts and too self-absorbed.

RB: Did you ever feel that you were not treated the same as a man?

AR: Of course, especially in the workplace, where it could be particularly unpleasant. I stopped working in graphics because it became too compromising. I knew I could never become an editor, and I was expected to provide other services, if you know what I mean. I left because I couldn't stand being treated that way.

RB: What about the artists' unions?

AR: There were no gender problems there. I know that we were supposed to be equal, but we weren't. We were expected to work like a man and also run the family. We worked very hard. But in truth the men were also degraded. The problem was not so much our oppression as their degradation under the Soviet regime. Women had to deal with everyday realities, including putting up with the government. When a child was born, the government would send hyperbolic praises to you. "We congratulate you on the birth of a new protector of our motherland." They really butted into our private lives. Yet we tried to preserve a private existence. Men did not have such options. If they could not provide for their families or maintain a sense of their own individuality, they got into personal trouble. Drunkenness is not a national characteristic, but it is a problem because of our social situation. All our men are underdeveloped. They are infantile and are not self-realized. That is why it is so amusing to hear questions about feminism. We have other problems. Perhaps soon we will have a desire to become feminists. But first one has to know what it means to be a woman. A woman in this country has one role—that is motherhood. In this country, she can only be a mother. And in relationship to men, she is still a mother.

RB: Do you have a family?

AR: I have three children and I am divorced.

RB: Was your divorce due to the fact that you are an artist?

AR: I think so. It is assumed that with three children you stay home. My husband was a nice man. He helped me physically, but something was missing in the relationship. I was the one with the calling. He was simply there. He had no desire to accomplish anything. He let things ride. Even our circle of friends was uncomfortable with my ambitions. This complicated our relationship. There came a time when I found it much simpler to be on my own than to feel guilty all the time.

RB: Do you have supportive friends?

AR: I changed friends after my divorce, so I can't say that I have a circle of support. But I have an inner necessity and a sense of obligation to myself. I have to work and I don't know why. I cannot live a quiet life.

RB: Has life been difficult these past few years?

AR: I have personal problems that have no relationship to events. Personally, I searched for something and I believe that I have found it. So I feel sure of myself. My search is to find my own expressive language. But the situation is terrible for our children. We are fearful for them. I fear for their physical and emotional well-being. I have no money, and I always live without money. This is nothing new, but it is more serious now. In the past, our social structure functioned without money. But not now. Money is destroying us more than the Soviet regime did.

RB: How can you still work?

AR: I feel that I have a lot of potential. People think I am very strong, but I don't know.

RB: Does the word *feminist* mean anything to you?

AR: I'm afraid I don't know what a "feminist" means. But something in the feminist program interests me. I did go to a feminist conference in London a few years ago. I found the English feminists boring, shallow, with no depth, cartoonlike. But I'm now beginning to see our culture with new eyes. For the last, oh, I don't know how many years, culture has been constructed by men. We see things through a masculine consciousness. Understanding this came as a revelation to me. So I'm grateful to feminists who called this to my attention. I came from a family of independent women. My grandmother and mother were emancipated women. All my life I have fought against so-called masculine behavior. I have fought for such a long time that I behave like a man. I instinctively respond negatively to any question about feminism. But I do live like a feminist. I guess I don't want to admit it. To be a feminist means that I have to be totally responsible for all decisions, to be accountable for everything. Well, I guess I'm a feminist.

RB: Let's push this a little bit. Does your inner voice come from your experiences as a woman?

AR: I'm a person who thinks about ideas. I don't think that women in general do that. I have intellectual inclinations and I am prone to an analytic approach in my work. Women don't think that way. My thought processes are very male, independent, and tough. Women don't possess such qualities. But this is my image of myself.

RB: Do you like these qualities in a man?

AR: I don't think so. What I like is sensitivity, understanding. I don't like aggression, yet I am an aggressive person. I don't know where it comes from. Perhaps it's a defense mechanism.

RB: What about your art?

AR: A painting starts in my subconscious and then I begin a conscious process. Here is a painting of a drowned woman, a mermaid. At first, mermaids were alive, but once they drowned they became demonic characters. This theme haunted me and I couldn't understand why. It is a folkloric theme, but it seemed to be the right sort of expression. Perhaps I had a feeling that I was drowning. Clearly, this was an escape fantasy, an escape from my problems. As a drowned corpse, I fantasized that I would become evil. It was a feeling of the lack of freedom. It was a sloughing off of my problems as a woman. I was in a situation in which I thought I was drowning, although I really don't like it when the personal spills over into your work.

RB: Is there any connection to the contemporary scene?

AR: I think we are building one large Potemkin Village, a cardboard village, which can come apart with the poke of a finger.

RB: I see in some of your work you quote Velázquez and other old masters [fig. 16]. Why?

AR: I'm not certain. But I'm interested in the body. There are two things here. There's a grid and there's a straight line. I read into a woman's body a straight line, a line much stronger than I find in a man's body. The female line is more natural, and that interests me. I was curious to see

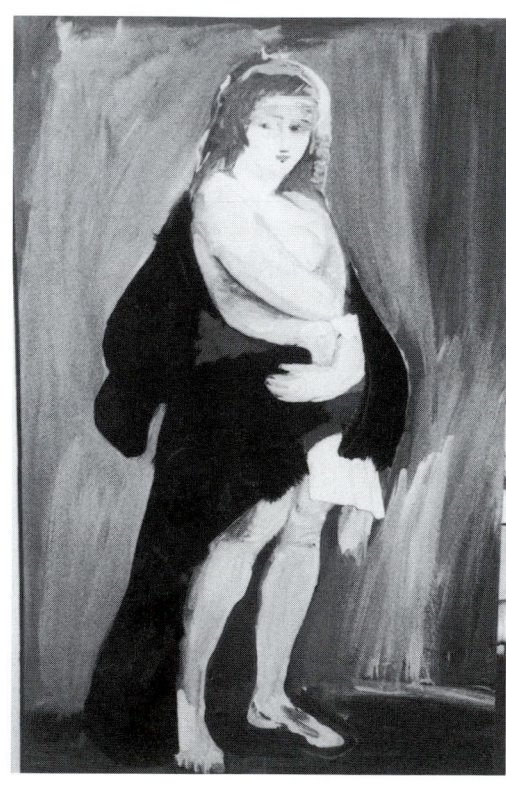

16. Alena Romanova, *After Rubens*, 1995, oil on canvas. (Courtesy Alena Romanova.)

how the old masters worked with lines. I also love old pictures, but I'm somewhat removed from them. So I tried to reestablish contact with them. This picture I called *Rubens's Fur Coat.*

RB: What do you think Rubens was trying to express?

AR: I'm not entirely certain, but the viewer should be stirred by what she sees. I have tried to experience what is in Rubens's paintings

RB: An American would say that these works were originally painted by men and that you are reclaiming the female body for women.

AR: I have to think about that. First, I would have to say that a woman's body is much more interesting to paint than a man's. It is irrational, I know, but there is an intense sensual pleasure in painting the female nude. Second, there is quite a bit of irony here, since men used the female nude exclusively as an object for painting. Therefore, I would agree that I am trying to equal the score. This interests me because male artists have treated the female body as if it were a flower instead of a person.

RB: I see you have made your versions of several Rubens paintings— *The Rape of Europa, The Abduction of the Daughters of Leocippus.*

AR: I tried to be playful. What happens when you remove some figures from a picture? It is a game with art—to see how the old masters organized and constructed their pictures. And again, the female body is more sensual than the male body. I have no interest in having sex with a woman. Rather, I see the body as a landscape. There are hills, valleys. I don't understand how to paint a male body. The male body is suited for war, and I have no interest in war. A female body possesses passion. I might paint a male body someday, since I am interested in the Narcissus myth. Maybe a warrior. But a male body resembles an animal. You have to give him a shield and sew on patches. Otherwise, he is not self-sufficient. A woman's body is self-sufficient.

Alena Martinova

Alena Martinova (b. about 1965) was the only artist we were able to interview who uses her own body, sometimes naked, in her performance pieces. She was the most transgressive and least inhibited artist we met, and although some of her work may or may not be derived from earlier American and European examples (to be discussed later), it served and probably still serves the purpose in Russia of suggesting what is possible if traditional ways of thinking are abandoned. This interview was given in 1998.

AM: Usually, Moscow women find some theme for themselves and stay with that theme. For a while, I suffered from a split personality. I mean that I was busy painting very modest pictures, religious icons, and at the same time acting in performances using my body. I also tried to write some articles. But now, I am concentrating on body art and trying not to lose courage in what I do. I'll try anything. Just yesterday, I went to a TV program, "Twelve Decisive Women," where Vladimir Zhirinovsky, the nationalist, was appearing. He said the ideal woman cries, knits, and loves. I went up to him and told him that I was his ideal woman because I cry a lot and can learn how to embroider. And then few days ago I did a two-act performance called *Sade de Sade.* A striptease, *Justine,* ran parallel. [*Justine,* a novel by the marquis de Sade, is about a young woman who, through a series of misadventures, dies.] My story was about the suffering in my life and the scars I have to show for it. I inflicted on myself superficial scars, including opening a vein, and also being scarred during an orgasm. Another part was about swimming across the Volga River, where I fell under a boat. I wanted to nurse people there. I had all kinds of scars on my breasts and wanted to give my heart to children. Eagles picked at my liver. I was in such agony that I wanted to commit suicide. This was pure art. I did not undress during this performance. This took place at one of the clubs in Moscow where you can have art performances.

RB: How do you explain your interest in body art?

AM: I realized that as a painter I had reached an impasse. My pictures were too lyrical, and, anyway, I do not have a studio nor do I have the means to paint. So I tried a different venue for my creative energies. I am not ashamed to be a female clown, a vampire. In fact, I left home when I was fourteen to begin to work in the theater in Kishinev [in Moldavia]. I also had some professional training there as a painter from 1981 to 1985. I then ran off to Moscow, but did not have a permit to stay. So I went to Yaroslav [in central Russia northeast of Moscow], where I continued my art training. I learned how to make dolls and puppets. I was constantly sought by the police, since I didn't have documentation at first. So I went to school. Finally, I graduated from a theater institute and was assigned by the government to go to a small town in the Yaroslav region. I was to work on a farm, which would have been suicidal. I then went to Moscow to say good-bye to my friends. A homosexual acquaintance proposed marriage so that I could stay in Moscow. We married on April Fools' Day.

RB: In your travels, were you treated as equally as men?

AM: In Moscow, I began to meet men in the avant-garde world and men in the art union. The latter would shout at me, "Where are you going? Stay put and paint still lifes. Don't push yourself on us!" Perhaps they saw me as a competitor, since I was ambitious and pushy.

RB: Well, did you feel oppressed?

AM: I have felt oppressed since childhood because I'm a smart aleck. I manage to be in conflict with everybody, probably because I am fearless. I have a bad reputation. I am also not afraid of my body, although I had a puritanical upbringing. I am not ashamed to show myself nude. People ask how I can paint icons in a church environment and also disrobe. I say that God created us naked. What difference does it make if you show an arm or a leg or your entire body?

RB: When did you first begin body performances?

AM: The first one, a video, was for the Telegalery, called *The Completion of the Phrase and the Technology of a Radical Gesture.* In it a man is shaving his private parts and his chest. Suddenly, we see a woman's genitalia, a total change. In a parallel video, we showed somebody drawing doves on a man's shaved pubic region. To change the subject, I once actually had a conversation with Gorbachev. During the election campaign in 1996, I tried to talk to all the major candidates. I had the idea that I was pursuing a grand amour, a grand love. After all, the politicians were handsome and such great men, and I, a woman, was in search of love. I gave Gorbachev a piece of paper on which I drew some doves and slipped it into a magazine that I gave to him. It was shown on television, and I was seen squeezing his hand. I was creative in that I had created information that never existed before. I did a follow-up piece in which I appeared to be in love with all the candidates. I even went to press conferences. Then, in my fantasy, when they stop liking me, I attempt to kill the president. My picture got into a magazine with the announcement that I tried to kill the president. This, of course, was a game, to point out how information gets transmitted. My gimmick here was that I did the traditional female thing of appearing to be in love. But I took revenge for unrequited love. I became a tragic clown or a vamp. Afterward, I explored further politics and terrorism as themes. When I really asked at a lecture if Trotsky and the Mexican painter David Alfaro Siqueiros disliked each other more for personal than for political reasons and the audience shouted me down, I knew I was on to something. [Siqueiros had been involved in a plot to kill Trotsky in Mexico in the 1940s.] Nobody looks at the private lives of politicians as sources for their actions, so I grabbed this idea. I did a computer graphics piece called *Compromising Situation,* in which, using computer-montage effects, I seem to be in intimate situations with the country's leaders.

Since this sort of thing happens in real life, I decided to exploit the topic. In this way, I extracted a personal revenge on all politicians.

RB: Have you done more personal pieces?

AM: I also had plastic surgery that I turned into a performance. I did not do what Orlan has done [Orlan is the French artist whose performances include describing plastic surgery on her face as the surgery is taking place]. Right after my surgery, my face was plastered and threads were hanging from my nose. I looked frightening. I went to an opening of a show in this condition. Everybody looked at me, at my face. People asked what had happened. I told a feminist that my husband had broken my nose. I told a journalist that I was hit by a bullet. I also said that a gangster had cut off my nose, that I had syphilis, whatever. The next day, journalists called, wanting to write about my story. The truth is that I did have surgery, and I had friends with me during the operation and we chatted with each other.

RB: All of this for artistic reasons?

AM: The first operation was done to repair a broken nose. I made it the subject of a performance called *The Dancing Divinity*. The idea was that humans changed from monkeys to humans quickly and had plastic surgery on their noses. I did the piece naked to convey an animal state that changes to a human state and ultimately into a divine state. I did this in 1989. The next year I injured my nose and needed a second operation. I turned that into a continuous performance in my apartment as my nose healed. I did another piece called *My Personal Life Does Not Touch Me.* I appeared in a photo as a saint. There were little jars in front of it with my tears, my fingernail clippings, my hair, relics of sainthood. Behind little holes in the photo, you could see a video of everyday life proceeding in a normal way—guests visiting, food in the kitchen, somebody giving me a massage.

RB: Are there others doing similar work?

AM: Not really. I don't think there are any women who do performances as I do. I want to create myths about myself. One is that I am interested in prostitution. One piece, *Everything for Sale,* went on the Internet. I announced that my performance of fellatio is a work of art and my price is high because art is a luxury object. Anal sex comes much cheaper. Men took me seriously and began to make propositions. They objected to my prices. Women who responded knew I was playing a game; the men approached my piece in a very practical way.

RB: Are you working on any feminist pieces now?

AM: Bisexuality has become fashionable, so I have worked up a piece on Dracula's fiancée, and then on Frankenstein's bride. In my version, she reappears and we fall in love. This will lead to a third work with me as the bride of the Terminator. These women are basically lesbians. As the bride of the Terminator, I will appear out of the future in order to know earthly love. I will conceive a virtual baby and will be able to reconcile the world of people and the world of machines. I will appear to be very powerful in a reversal of gender roles.

RB: How do Russian men react to your activities?

AM: My husband works at the Telegalery. He thought *The Dancing Divinity* was all right, but not *Everything for Sale.* My very first performance was a video about shaving my pubic hair. We work collaboratively, but he does not know about everything I do.

In the video performance mentioned in the interview, *The Completion of the Phrase and the Technology of a Radical Gesture,* from the mid-1990s, Martinova shaved her pubic hair and then painted or has painted on the just shaved region multicolored flowers. She wanted to show women's vulnerability, to comment negatively on female beauty products, to indicate that women can do whatever they choose with their bodies, and to critique those who denigrate women as flower painters as well as those who think women are only concerned with hairstyles. Her husband collaborated in this performance because, as she said, "it is only when the husband begins to collaborate with the wife that he allows her to do something. A woman alone encounters barriers." She felt that she was in a damned-if-you-do-damned-if-you-don't situation in that she could not do certain things without help from a man. Nevertheless, her pieces certainly herald a new kind of freedom in Russia both in her actions as a woman and in the way she chooses to present herself. To borrow a phrase used to describe the works of American performance artist and feminist Carolee Schneemann, Martinova engages in "self-conscious actions that insist on the centrality of a woman producing her own image."[3] That is, she is an image maker creating her own self-image. She also exhibits a degree of narcissism unthinkable in Soviet times.

Martinova, in mentioning Orlan's name, revealed an awareness of Western performance artists. Although not a performance artist, Linda Lovelace shaved her pubic hair in the Amereican movie *Deep Throat,* which dates from the early 1970s. We were also present, in 1971, when the American Fluxus artist Geoffrey Hendricks shaved his body hair in a performance called *Body/Hair,* in which he shaved all of his body hair and put it into small jars labeled with the area from which it came (e.g., left armpit, right thigh). But finding antecedents of which Martinova might or might not be aware is irrelevant here. The important point is that she has been on the further fringes of the Moscow art world helping to create a climate of opinion in which equally adventurous artists can function and flourish.

We met another performance artist in St. Petersburg, Natalia Pershina-Yakimanskaia (b. 1969), who explores in her work the changes wrought by the collapse of Soviet rule. An early piece, done in Stockholm in 1988 when she was only nineteen years old, reflects the state of mind of many artists around that time. They critiqued and revealed their anger about, and their impatience with, the old system, and they expressed their hopes, facing an unpredictable future in which change was now a possibility. Disappointment set in soon after, by the early 1990s, but Pershina-Yakimanskaia's piece recalls that earlier mood and can be read as a signature statement of the optimism people that then felt. The piece, which she performed with one other woman, was concerned with the desire for a real experience (of love, of life) at the borderline of death and self-annihilation (fig. 17). The two women threw themselves around the performance area, which was strewn with garbage. They cut up their clothing and ate strawberries, among other activities. Ultimately, they died, longing for something good to happen. Pershina-Yakimanskaia's intention was to explore new sets of parameters between love and death as the old limits and old thoughts were being destroyed.

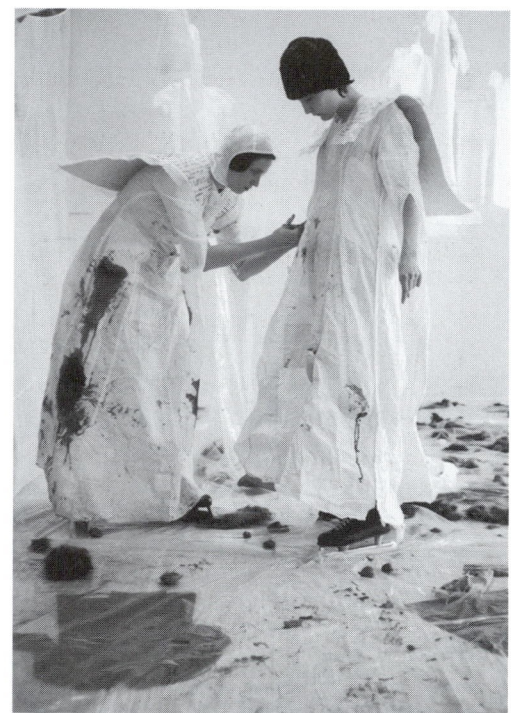

17.   Natalia Pershina-Yakimanskaia, *Love and War,* 1988, performance. (Courtesy Natalia Peshina-Yakimanskaia.)

Elena Kitaeva

Elena Kitaeva (b. early 1960s) also explored women's retributive fantasies in a few pieces. But she is in no way as improbable or as reckless as Martinova. Rather, she is a successful commercial designer and lives in a new, elegant apartment house with her graphics-artist husband. She also uses the male body in her art, one of the few who does so. This interview was given in 1998.

RB: Where did you go to school?

EK: I was born near Moscow, but grew up in Minsk. I went to the Academy of Art and Design there and graduated in 1986.

RB: How were you treated?

EK: We were five girls in a class of about thirty. When you entered the upper grades, there was discrimination. Boys were given preferential treatment by being given higher grades and evaluations. The authorities did not like girl students, but in acting school, the reverse was true.

RB: How did all this manifest itself?

EK: On the day a girl is born, there is a lot of sniggering. With a boy, the parents are congratulated. We all know this. At school, I was an A student, but I was not popular. I guess other pupils do not like an A student, but my teachers were encouraging and predicted a successful future for me. They liked girls who showed talent and application. So when such a girl appeared, they welcomed her.

RB: And your family?

EK: Everybody was pleased with me. I married in Minsk and came to Moscow with my husband. He is a well-known graphic artist.

RB: How did you support yourself?

EK: I am both a designer and an artist. As an artist, I use the name Mao. I use my own name for my designs. I earn money as a designer, which supports my art.

RB: Why do you use the nude male form [fig. 18]?

EK: I worked on a theme called *The Deck of Cards* based on works from the 1920s and 1930s. I know that was a terrible time—concentration camps, government terror. But people were basically ordinary, honest, and pure. I made a deck of cards with jacks, kings, and queens, really faces of pilots, workers, and girls on collective farms, and slowly they grew into reliefs, some gigantic.

RB: Why mostly male bodies?

EK: There was a cult of the body. You know that later we had a cult of personality in the Soviet Union, and the physical body was shunned. It

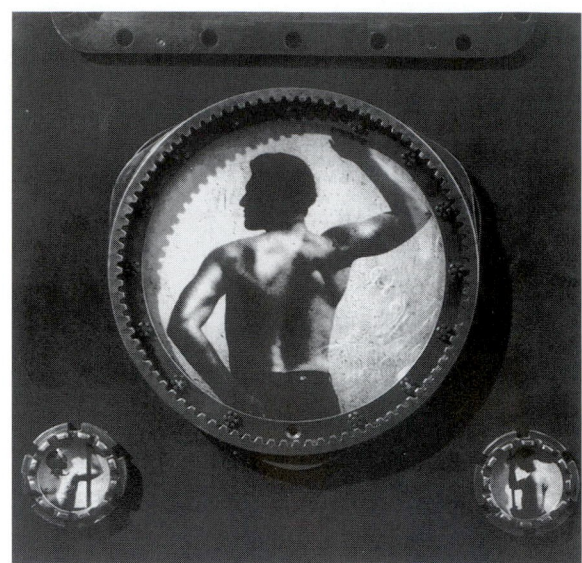

18. Elena Kitaeva, *Athlete,* 1995, oil. (Courtesy Elena Kitaeva.)
....

was considered more prestigious to be concerned with the mind. But during the 1920s and 1930s, there was an interest in the body, as well. The fascists and the Communists both had a certain admiration for physical beauty.[4] Today, the body is a subject in the West. Here in Russia there is a tendency to see the body in neoclassical terms. So the body is a good image to work with. The chief representative of this tendency is Timor Novikov, who lives in St. Petersburg. He is contributing to a renaissance in classical art, bringing an old style into contemporary form. After *The Deck of Cards,* I did a piece called *The Young Maiden and Death.* Any artist admires beautiful, classical works of art, gorgeous nudes, wonderful proportions. There is no ideology here, only the artistic gaze.

RB: Is this a response to Soviet prudery?

EK: Well, we have all suffered from the years we lost because of the regime. We have a negative relationship with those days [see interview with Ludmila Gorlova]. There was a moment in the early 1990s when we thought that everything associated with that time was bad, evil. But then we thought there must have been something good from those times. What was good was the young people, the developed, well-proportioned body.

RB: Are there women's organizations in Moscow?

EK: No. I think that serious women who accomplish something in literature and the arts will hardly unite as a group. They are very powerful individuals and personalities and would hardly organize themselves. But I know of a group called Duma that is concerned with practical matters such as child care. I am friendly with young, serious women who have achieved something in their lives. We are not loud or flashy, and we know one another. I am especially friendly with Renata Litvinova, who is an actress, writer, and director. We prepared a piece for a recent Woman's Day event. It was dedicated to the way women can be both victims and killers at the same time, but more of the latter. The piece embodies all the myths of famous women killers, such as Lucretia Borgia, who also committed suicide. The project concerned the apotheosis of women. The woman appears as fatal to the man and decides his fate, but she does not necessarily live.

RB: Do you find much competition between men and women?

EK: No. Women are spiritually united against men because they underestimate our capabilities. We can be original, create original things, and men do not behave well toward us. At exhibitions, you can see that some women are just stronger artists. But women often avoid battles with men. They just drop out. We are more vulnerable.

RB: Do you compete with your husband?

EK: During bad periods, we sometimes have to clarify our relationship. He will tell me that he has spent too much energy helping me with my career. But this rarely happens. We are really good friends. It is much easier in our country if we have friendly relations with our spouses. Many of us work in pairs and if we are successful, we are much better off than people who work alone.

RB: Do you have incidents in which you feel discrimination?

EK: All the time. Even now I am constantly rocking the boat, demanding my rights. At times, men in charge are at a lower rung and less educated than I am. But they are men, so they think, "We can't let her talk." I scream. I yell. I have to. Most successful women do the same. We all have reputations. I am actually a very nice, soft person, but I have a reputation for being a madwoman. If you don't scream at full voice, nobody will listen to you. On the other hand, it is acceptable for a man to scream. In our culture, such men are highly regarded and pampered. My general understanding of men is this: they are weak. Women do everything and things come out the way we want them to. Women are the heads of families. They tell everybody where to stand to and where to sit. Many men are under our thumbs, but we allow them to appear independent. I even boss my husband around sometimes, but he is a deep, quiet man, a very generous person.

RB: Do you have role models?

EK: My mother. She is strong and had a responsible job. She encouraged me to be strong. I don't know if I could have managed as well without her example. Because of her, I never had any doubts. The road was open to me. I think that if a woman wants to achieve anything in Russia, she can. Nobody has set up serious boundaries. My husband and I had a show in Japan in 1998. People commented that even though I am a woman, my work was strong and masculine. Even abroad, people could see the difference between my work and the work of some young man that might be weak.

There are four points Kitaeva makes that other interviewees made repeatedly. First, their mothers, especially if they were remembered as strong women, served as role models. Second, the artists wanted their work to appear as if it had been done by a man or to project masculine rather than feminine qualities, the latter being a term of disparagement. That is, good quality was associated with masculinity, however the word was defined. Third, women, especially women strong in character, do not want to organize. Fourth, there is an acknowledgment of a battle between the sexes—which, depending on the couple, might remain playful or become antagonistic. It is also clear that Kitaeva is self-assured and is well aware of that personality trait in herself. In order to exercise that self-assurance, she is forced to be aggressive, even irritating, to men with whom she works. That is, her assumption of leadership roles is not guaranteed by talent, which would be more the case if she were a man, but it is facilitated by her willingness to do battle if necessary. Elena Figurina, probably the most successful women artist from St. Petersburg, told us that she, too, has been able to assume certain roles because of her aggressive personality (see interview).

In the following few interviews, we want to consider husband-wife relationships, to which Kitaeva alluded. Three of the more explosive interviews—with Helena Heinrihsone of Riga, Latvia, Larissa Zvezdochetova of Moscow; and Viktoria Buivid of St. Petersburg—follow Figurina's.

Elena Figurina

Elena Figurina (b. 1955), originally trained as an engineer, is a self-taught, internationally exhibited painter from St. Petersburg. A former dissident artist, her soft-focused, melancholic, and androgenous figures belie her no-nonsense personality (fig. 19). We interviewed her twice, most recently in 1995.

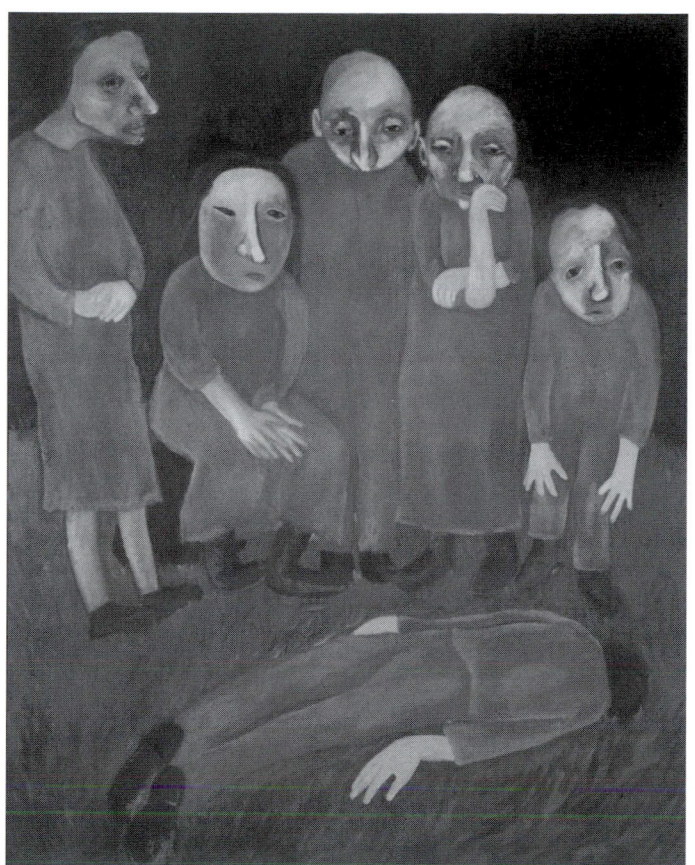

19. Elena Figurina, *Return of the Prodigal Son,* 1987, oil on canvas. (Courtesy of Jane Voorhees Zimmerli Art Museum, Rutgers, The State University of New Jersey. Gift of Barbara J. Hazard.)

EF: When I began to paint, we had other problems—political, economic—so that gender did not matter. We were all part of the opposition.

RB: Have you experienced any discrimination since?

EF: If a person is sure of himself and works independently and doesn't allow mistreatment, then everything is surmountable. But, I have come up against some discrimination. Recently, an artist recommended me to a new museum formed by artists. The organizers, in a huff, asked, "Who is she? We don't admit women." These were artists who had belonged to the union. So I stayed away from them.

RB: And in life?

EF: I have no children, so I can work uninterruptedly. It is impossible to have a career and a family. You can't split yourself in two. It is either one or the other. I am totally immersed in my work, and my life just turned out that way. Women whom I knew when I started painting now have families. They can't do anything else except run the household. I feel sorry for them. From the original group I was friendly with, I am the only women still around who paints full-time.

RB: You are very independent.

EF: A bit late in my life, but it's OK. As a rule, men organize big events, but I was always part of an organizing group. For instance, in the 1980s, we had an association of unofficial (dissident) artists. Of the 140 artists, they elected a leadership committee of 7. I was the only woman in that group. I was always at the helm of the organizers. I know it is in my personality. My nature is to be a leader. I knew how to be one and I had no problems, except once. We were approached by an American to mount an exhibition in 1988. The stipulation was that there had to be a fifty-fifty split between men and women. The men were opposed and I was for it. Since the American was a woman, we had the fifty-fifty split. Men do like power, but I also like being part of an organizing group because I like interacting with male artists. Usually, they do not consider women worthy enough to discuss art or art organizations. Perhaps there have been too few women artists or maybe the men lack a certain kind of socialization. All of this forced me to try to be at the center of things. Women were usually barred, but I kept pushing and I was able to get into leadership roles. I was able to make decisions.

RB: Are you in touch with any feminist groups in St. Petersburg?

EF: No. I once participated in a women's group show. But feminism is quite new to us and we don't quite know what to do with it. Honestly, I look at it critically and do not want to participate. Let me tell you how it first manifested itself here. We began to see some feminists in the late 1970s. What I saw parading as feminists were women who came to openings and bared their breasts to nurse their babies. This was an act of feminism. So we have not yet unified to support one another. But some women are organizing. Art exhibitions are essential to us, and women are often overlooked. So we are beginning to organize our own shows. We know exactly who the enemy is.

Helena Heinrihsone

Helena Heinrishone (b. 1948) lives in Riga, Latvia. She and her artist husband occupy a large, top-floor loft space near the Old City. Her work, composed of large, bright areas of color, is semi-abstract in style (fig. 20). Like other interviewees, she was not aware of feminist or gender issues, but some of her paintings could fit easily into a feminist art exhibition. Her conversation suggested that she was fed up with current male-female relationships, but she nevertheless was obviously pleased to show us her husband's work. This interview was given in 1995, but was updated in 1998 when Heinrihsone was in New York.

RB: Were you born in Latvia?

HH: Yes, in Riga. But my family is a mixture. My father was a Cossack. Perhaps that is why I like bright colors, but I think of myself as a cosmopolitan person. I studied at the art academy here and finished in 1973. There were always more girls in my classes. I never experienced any discrimination as a woman either at school or in exhibiting, but conditions are bad now. The government used to support us. Before the fall of the Soviet Union, our profession was very prestigious. It was something special. Now, we have to earn a living.

RB: Was your family supportive?

HH: Yes. My grandmother, who was very well educated, gave me a book on Picasso when I was about ten years old.

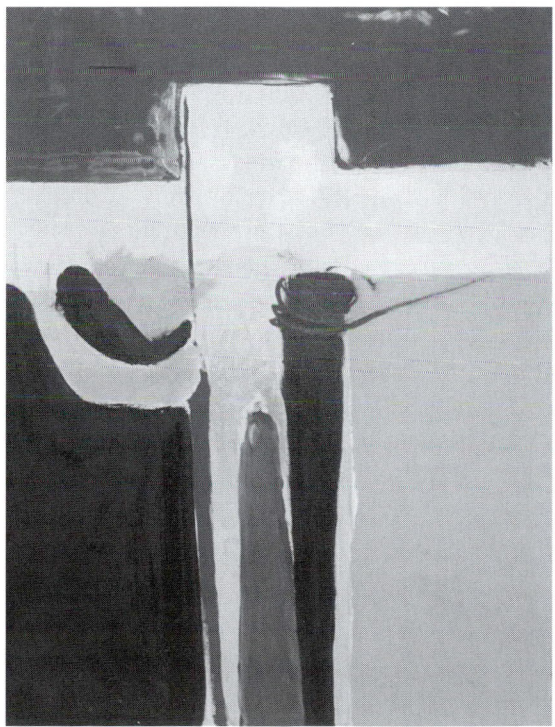

. . . .

2 0. Helena Heinrihsone, *Woman Crucified*, 1995, acrylic on canvas. (Courtesy Helena Heinrihsone.)

RB: Tell me about your teachers.

HH: There were more male teachers. I preferred studying with a male. As in going to a church, one wants a male priest.

RB: Can you tell a painting done by a man or by a woman?

HH: Yes. I believe that women are more sensitive. I'm working on a painting now that has a half-woman-half-cat in it. The creature warms itself by the fire. I believe a man wouldn't paint such a picture, because he is not in touch with his feelings. The difference is in the theme. Styles are not so different between men and women.

RB: Do you think your artistic voice comes from your experiences as a woman?

HH: Yes. When I know what I want to express, then I have a rush of feelings. I paint from my experiences, from my sufferings and the sufferings of my friends. I painted a picture called *Woman Crucified* [see fig. 20]. I thought that if Christ is the symbol of suffering, then there should not be any difference whether it is a man or a woman, because women also suffer. I came to this subject when I was commissioned to paint a picture for a church altar. When I submitted it, it caused a scandal and it was rejected. I really do think that women suffer more than men. I had many discussions with a Lutheran minister, especially when I began reading the Bible in preparation for the painting. I wanted to prove to him that my portrayal of Christ as a suffering woman should not make any difference. I still don't understand the rejection. If we consider that Christ on the cross suffered, then he must have completed his mission of redemption. So what is the big deal? How many hours was he on the cross? When you compare this with the suffering of women under the Soviet regime, women who had to suffer abortions without anesthesia, the moral trauma—can you compare it? This was how I argued with the priest. Besides, I thought, if he will save and redeem humanity from suffering, so what is it to have been hanging on the cross for a few hours? Not so terrible. I didn't want to see a suffering Jesus on the cross, but a strong one who had accomplished his mission, his duty. I did another picture of Adam and Eve. He's weak and doesn't know where he's going because he's guilty by his own actions for having taken the apple. He should not have accused Eve. She offered it and he did not have to take it. So, he is weaker than she. Also, I don't think it was such a big sin to deserve expulsion. I have just begun to read the Bible, so I'm still unfamiliar with it. There is a look of horror on Eve's face in my painting. I read that there was a fire, so they could not return to paradise. I included the fire in my painting because I like the color red.

RB: Are you Lutheran?

HH: No. I wasn't even baptized. Lately, a friend has been talking to me about the Russian Orthodox Church. There I don't have to study to be baptized like in the Lutheran Church.

RB: I was wondering because I noticed some Orthodox elements in your work, such as the use of gold. Do you have time to paint?

HH: More or less. I take care of the household, but my husband understands that I am not so interested in house chores. We also have a daughter in her early twenties now. He was helpful in raising her. But the idea of equality doesn't work. The men pay no attention to women.

RB: Do you think empathy is a feminine characteristic?

HH: I believe so. My husband paints very fast, but I need time to contemplate a picture, to dwell with it and experience it. Men are stronger physically and they can concentrate longer than women. But I have more obligations around the apartment. I'll be cooking while I'll also be thinking of a picture. Men are more compartmentalized. When they cook, they cook, and when they paint, they paint. They can only do one thing at a time. Women are more universal. We have a greater capacity for combining different tasks. I am always looking for time to paint. I can't sit in my bathrobe and read the newspaper for two hours in the morning like he does.

Larissa Zvezdochetova

Larissa Zvezdochetova (b. 1958) was the most intense, angry artist we interviewed. She is one of the few artists who has tried to forge an art from craft forms associated with women. Yet, like others, she wants no part of a feminist movement in the art world. We met her in her studio with her third husband, a Swedish man in the diplomatic service, who remained quiet throughout the interview, but, through his body language, was very supportive. This interview was given in 1995.

RB: Does your art grow from your experiences as a woman?

LZ: I am certain of it. Male artists do not seriously consider women as artists, that we are capable of making art, because women do not possess similar intellectual levels of understanding. They believe that intellectual pursuits are a male privilege, that only men can deal with such matters. They present themselves as all-knowing and always right. Most men think this way probably because there are so few women artists in Russia, especially in our circle [this being experimental, radical]. There were women in the artists' unions, but as a rule they were relegated to the departments of applied arts, which included tapestry, weaving, and ceramics. The women in our circle include Maria Sere-briakova, Elena Elagina, Mila Skripina, Olga Chernisheva. There is also a local group called Pertsi, which has five women and about two hundred men. Clearly, a numerical imbalance, and the men occupy all the privileged positions.

RB: And discrimination?

LZ: Inequality exists from the very start. And today I feel wildly diminished as a person and as an artist when I am invited to participate in all-women shows. It is a humiliation to be in special women's shows, as if these were for some national or sexual minorities.

RB: In America, we have galleries that often feature feminist art.

LZ: We are just beginning to become familiar with feminist issues. I understand that you have already established a tradition of women fighting for their rights. Not with us. Our mentality is that men have to work and that women, in the Eastern tradition, should sit at home with the children. This is basic. I have friends who live that kind of life. I'll call up and ask them to go to a movie, and they'll say that they cannot leave the children with their husbands because their husbands cannot do anything in the house. The children will go hungry and will not go to bed on time. What I am saying is that the women do not want to change. They like that kind of life. They are neither ambitious nor want to do something for themselves on the one hand and have their husbands share in family responsibilities on the other. I had a husband, Konstintin Zvezdochetov, an artist. We had a horrible problem because we are both artists. First, he treated me like a servant, a maid. My job was to take care of him. When he wanted to eat, he would say, "I want to eat." It was absurd. "I want lemonade. Go buy it." He expected me to be submissive. We were in constant battle. He was also envious that I had more money than he, that I sold more works. When people came over, he would show only his works and generally would forget about me. Once for a big show in Boston in 1990, David Ross [then the director of the Institute of Contemporary Art in Boston] visited us with Margarita Tupitsyn, the show's curator, to pick some works for the exhibition. My husband showed his paintings. I was running around, preparing food, making tea, acting like a hostess. He did not introduce me and nobody asked my name. I was like a piece of furniture. David Ross discovered that I was a painter and a good one. He was astonished. He noticed my work by sheer accident. He was looking around and saw some pieces and asked about them. I said they were mine. He took some for the exhibition. Again, let me say, this happened by sheerest chance.

RB: Was your husband envious?

LZ: All the time. He even demanded that we have a child and that I should take care of it while he would still be able to run around and enjoy himself. I decided that I did not want such a life. Actually, I had a miscarriage. After that, I decided that Kostia was not somebody I could depend on to help me out. So I never got pregnant again. I was afraid to be alone with a baby.

RB: You seem to be very strong.

LZ: I always had to struggle. My father was the first man I had to fight with. He had a very strong love for me, and still does. He was jealous of my boyfriends and would get sick when they came to see me. My first step to independence was to get married. I was strong-headed and immature. I was only seventeen. Everything in my parents' house conspired to keep me there, so I knew I had to flee. Still, I wanted his approval, but I have not yet got it. He was a jeweler, but wanted to be a painter. He therefore wanted to realize his ambitions through me. Unfortunately, our creative aspirations and ideologies are different, and we could not really communicate, and we still cannot.

RB: Tell me about your development as an artist.

LZ: I'm from Odessa and studied graphic arts at the Pedagogical Institute there. I finished in 1982. I was prepared to be a teacher.

RB: What about your classes?

LZ: There were many boys and few girls. I had two wonderful women teachers to whom I owe a lot. Generally speaking, I think that women are better suited to educate students. They are not as focused as men and can give a better humanistic education. They will discuss art, dance, cinema, everything.

RB: Did the teachers pay more attention to the boys?

LZ: No. Boys as a rule painted better from nature, but the girls painted better pictures.

RB: Did you exhibit anywhere?

LZ: In Odessa at some women's shows. Nothing important. I didn't begin to work seriously until I moved to Moscow in 1988. Vadim Zakharov shared a studio with five men, and since I was Kostia's wife, I was able to join them. At first, I would bring dinner and fuss in the kitchen. When the guys left, I would begin to do my own work. When they would go abroad, then I could really spread out. I made no demands, since I was a guest. It was pleasant to meet, to socialize, and to discuss issues there. In time, I felt I needed my own space. I needed my own room, my own world. With the guys, it was always difficult. No matter what I would do, they would say that it was feminine art. They never considered my work seriously. I developed an incredible anger, and I thought that if they keep talking about women's art, then I will do women's art. I'll show them. So I searched for a theme that would deal specifically with women. My first painting was an imitation of needlepoint. Something women have always done. They sat and embroidered or did needlepoint or wove. I painted strips of thread on a canvas to give it the look of needlepoint, a textured look, to confuse the viewer. I also pasted on pieces of woven material. By imitating needlepoint, I wanted to make a statement. I wanted to make women's art. Actually, what I did then and do now is very kitchy.

RB: Are there sources for your work?

LZ: In Odessa, I worked at the National Center for the Arts, a place where amateurs worked with master-artists of the applied arts. An extraordinary women there, an invalid and a war veteran, did needlepoint. She worked from reproductions of great art, and recreated them using the cheapest threads she could find. Her colors were very bright. I decided that I wanted to make these same kinds of transformations of the original objects. Since union artists did not reflect reality in their works, and these amateurs at least reflected the taste of the times as well as a folk tradition, I decided to make use of that approach and general attitude. I decided to rehabilitate kitsch, since kitsch was always considered to be in bad taste. I was always accused of having bad taste. So I declared myself a person of bad taste, which implied a sort of banishment, a diminishment, an outcast status. But on the other hand, what is kitsch today might be considered good stuff in ten years' time.

RB: Do you consider this a feminine idea?

LZ: I would say so. As any mother would protect her child, so I will fight for my idea. I collected old things. After all, what is good taste or bad taste? Is liking Mickey Mouse bad taste? I looked around me on the street and in the neighborhood. I saw that we live in shit, in a dirty city. How could I develop good taste? If we drank tea from our teakettles, how could we discuss good taste? So I began to collect objects, the things we live with for a few years and then discard. I collect things that nobody wants anymore. I consider myself a contemporary archaeologist. I want to record the things that live with a person for a few years and then are thrown out. Insignificant things, like an empty pack of cigarettes, tickets, signs, become important witnesses to our cultural life. By contrast, ever since my childhood, the artists' unions have shown me that what we see in pictures does not represent reality or reflect our lives. Things that my friends now give me evoke tender feelings, even childhood associations and fantasies. I have paintings of plush carpets.

My father always thought that a home with a plush carpet is a home with bad taste. All my girlfriends had plush carpets in their homes. We did not. I thought they were splendid, and I would touch them when we visited. They seemed so cool and soft. I preserve these childhood experiences.

RB: What did your husband think of these pieces?

LZ: Kostia went abroad for six months in 1989. I worked very hard, and when he returned, I showed him my work. He paid no attention to what I had done. I was reduced to tears. He never said anything good about my work. In fact, the reverse is true. He would tear me down and tell everybody how awful my work was.

RB: What about the signs in your work and images of men [fig. 21]?

LZ: What can I say? Men are still my muses. They inspire me, even

. . . .

21. Larissa Zvezdochetova, *Mustard Plaster,* 1994, oil on canvas. (Courtesy Larissa Zvezdochetova.)

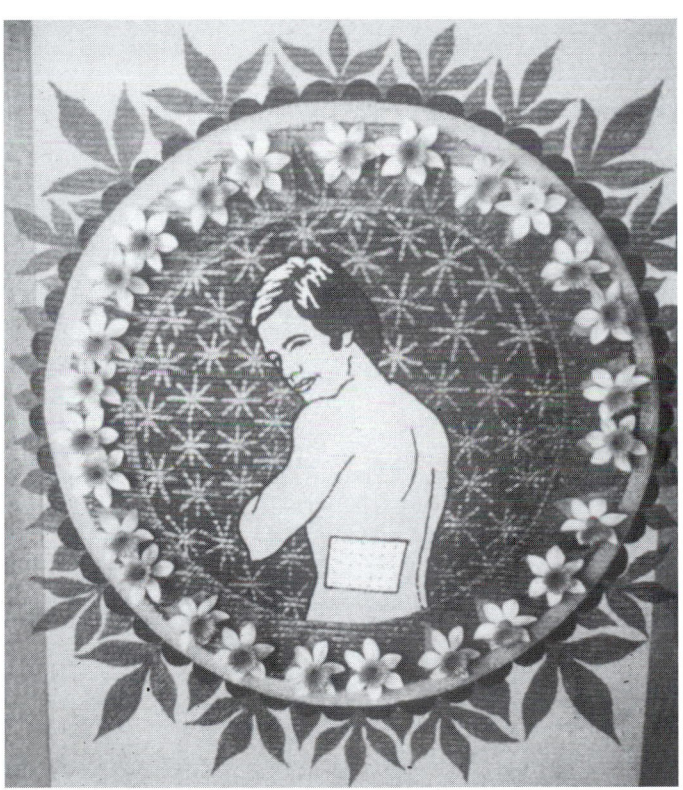

though I always quarrel with them. They are my friends. That is why I am always using male images in my work. I collect labels for wine bottles that have male images and want to use them on my carpets. I will dedicate them to all of my alcoholic friends. I stopped drinking, but they continue and think it is normal. I also discovered that labels carry images of women for household products, while entertainment images are usually male.

RB: What about friendships?

LZ: I prefer friendships with men, strange as it might seem. They are not always as supportive as I would like them to be. I have a reputation for scandalous behavior. Men are afraid of me. I am very protective of my rights and am very demanding now. So I create problems. It is better not to tangle with me. As a result, I don't feel any competition, now. I don't care what people think. I am self-sufficient, and won't conform to any standard.

RB: When you were growing up, did you feel you had equality?

LZ: No. On the daily level, there were always the questions of who would go shopping, clean up, take care of the house. Half of our lives are taken up running a household. Men, as a rule, rest and drink, have tea with friends, read the newspapers, watch TV; and women are supposed to cater to them. That is how things are here.

RB: Have conditions improved?

LZ: Not with men and not in our public lives. The government no longer purchases art, no longer commissions artists. Studios are being taken away and put on the open market. We did have an upsurge of shows from 1989 to 1993, but since then everything has slowed down [the situation right through to the end of the decade].

RB: What about feminism?

LZ: I don't think I am a feminist. I feel more that I am a type of Napoleon in female disguise. I am very ambitious. I have Napoleonic ambitions. It is everything or nothing. From childhood, I loved Napoleon. We are both small in size. People who are small want to be tall. They must have great ambition.

There are a few points worth considering here. First, like several other artists, Zvezdochetova, in effect, said that she can't live with men but that she does not want to live without them. Second, she acknowledges discrimination against women. Third, she is developing a women's art based, in part, on objects associated with women, but will have nothing to do with feminism because she finds it demeaning. Fourth, her work has affinities both to American pop art and Russian Sots art. With the former, she finds simplified images that appear to have been cycled through popular media. With the latter, she makes use of popular Russian objects in a serious, but also satiric, way. At the same time, she is a painterly painter in that her surfaces are richly textured to simulate the look and feel of carpets.

We should add here that we met one other artist, Marina Zhukova (b. 1960) from St. Petersburg who uses so-called women's art materials. One of her works, *Soft Monument: A Letter from the Front*, includes six sheets on which are sewn, among other things, a letter from her grandfather when he was fighting on the front in World War II (fig. 22). She said that she wanted to make a soft, intimate, and personal monument rather than a hard, government-sponsored, totalitarian one made from reinforced concrete. She has also worked with gloves.

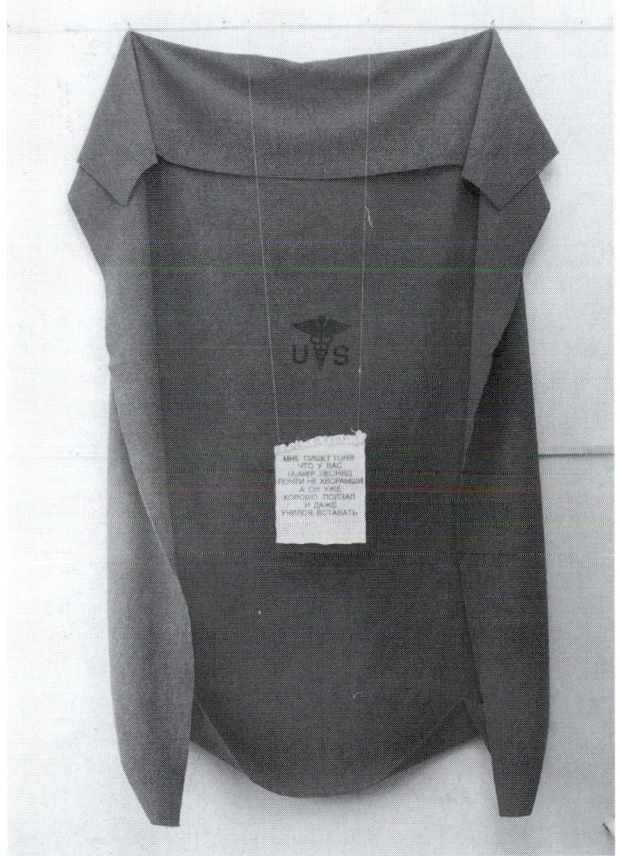

22. Marina Zhukova, *Blanket,* ca. 1995, blanket and paper. (Courtesy Marina Zhukova.)

Viktoria Buivid
....

Viktoria Buivid (b. early 1960s) is a photographer. She works with both male and female nudes, and with parts of bodies that stand for the entire figure. She sometimes sews details of photographs into shawls, gloves, and other garments and sundries (fig. 23). This interview was given in 1995.

> **RB:** Tell me about your schooling.
>
> **VB:** I grew up in Brezhnev's hometown, Dnepropetrovsk. It's in Ukraine, now. It was very provincial and politically oppressive, but culture was important there. There were a few more girls than boys in my classes and, as far as I can tell, no discrimination. But girls tended to be more obedient and were better students and enjoyed greater success in their earlier years. I went to a regular public school and then to an art high school. My parents, who are engineers, objected, thinking that artists are not normal people, that artists are no good. I had to quit art school. At the university, I studied philology, the standard course of studies for women. I gave my mother my diploma as a present.
>
> **RB:** When did you decide to become an artist?

....

2 3 .   Viktoria Buvid, *Shawl,* ca. 1995, photographs and shawl. (Courtesy Viktoria Buvid.)

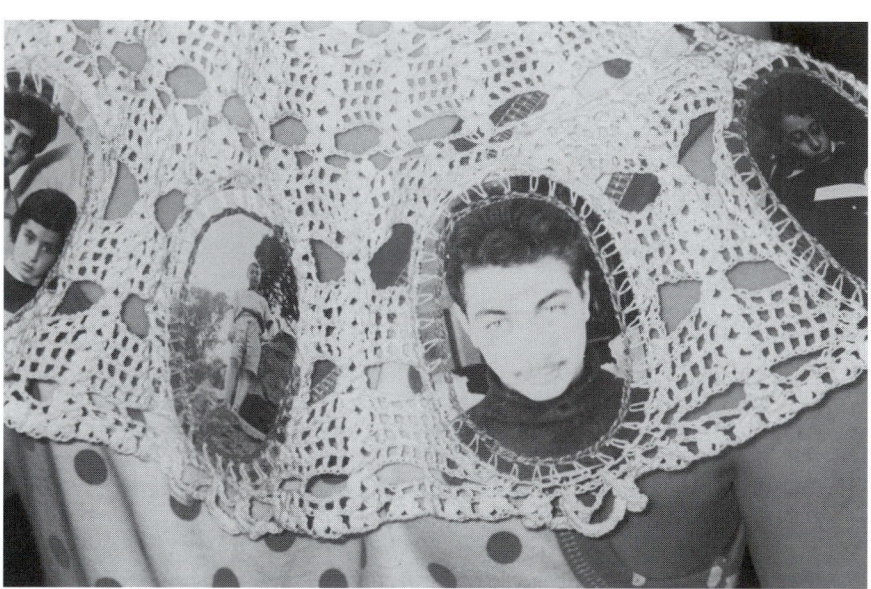

VB: It was in my personality. I was interested in all the arts from early childhood. In art school, we were treated equally and shared a common classical-academic education. We all learned to copy the same way. If we all went to the Nevskii Prospect [the main street in St. Petersburg] to paint people's portraits, they would all look the same.

RB: How were you evaluated?

VB: There were no distinctions. In our society, feminism is something new. We never heard of it. There was always equal pay for men and for women. Our situation is different and more difficult now. It is more important for us to work together with men to improve our conditions. Perhaps when life is normalized, we might enter into a struggle with them.

RB: Many women I interviewed, like yourself, had children at a young age.

VB: There are two main reasons. First, in our culture it is not acceptable for children to live apart from their parents. To escape, you get married. The second reason is medical. There are fewer complications and interferences from doctors when you give birth at twenty than when you do at thirty-five. It is not bad to be a young parent. You grow up together. My mother was thirty-eight when I was born, and we have a lot more problems than I do with my daughter. Also, one is still developing at twenty. You are not fully formed until you are about thirty, and you don't want to cut short your creative processes at that age. Thirty is not a good time to have a child. I would not want to have a child now. I would have no time for it.

RB: Did you marry an artist?

VB: Unfortunately, yes. Two artists in one family is one too many. I've been married twice, both times to photographers.

RB: Was there competition?

VB: It was something worse than competition with my first husband. It had to do with the birth of our child. We spent a lot of time with friends. As a new mother, I had to change my lifestyle in that I began to go to night school. I saw our friends less often as a result. This really did not suit me, so I got divorced. I decided before marriage that if I became unhappy, I would divorce. So we got divorced. With my second marriage, I had a different idea. Even if I became unhappy, I would stick it out. Everything went well until we moved to St. Petersburg from Poltava, the small town in Ukraine where we lived. My second husband wanted to immigrate to America—this was at the beginning of perestroika in 1990. I thought this was crazy, a fantasy. He spoke no English, but I knew enough of the language to fill out all of the forms. I didn't want to go because my fantasy was to live in St. Petersburg. So we moved there in 1990. And since this was in the time of perestroika, there was very little bureaucratic interference.

RB: What about your photography?

VB: In effect, my husband was my teacher. My photographs had mystical themes. Then, one day we found a trunk filled with things from the 1920s and 1930s—dresses and the like—that had clearly belonged to a ballerina. I photographed some of the fragile things she had. At that time, we met some Americans who were collecting photographs for an exhibition. I acted as translator for my husband, but I was also asked to submit about ten photos for their selection. Seven were chosen. Only five out of fifty of my husband's works were picked. He was not happy about that, since he had been my teacher and had taught me the basic technical aspects of photography, for which I am grateful. If the reverse had happened, I would have been happy for him. He went off in a sulk to his parents for two months. During that time, I enjoyed additional successes. When he returned, he actually stormed into the apartment; he demanded to see my work. It was all downhill after that. He found me disgusting to live with.

RB: Who supported you?

VB: My first husband would only visit to see our daughter. My second husband didn't bother at all. There were no support groups. But in 1990, Bela Matveeva and I began to work together with about four other women. We were all divorced and had had children at about the same age. We became one another's support. We would meet, drink tea, go to saunas, but nothing official, no regular get-togethers.

RB: What did you discuss?

VB: Never our private lives. I don't like explaining about bad husbands. We did not discuss our work either, because it is a custom here to do so primarily with critics and art historians. It is hard to explain. Any artist who experiences a moment of creativity does not want to discuss it until it is completely realized. Artists who do so are idiots and intellectual show-offs.

RB: Does your work come from your experiences as a woman?

VB: Yes. Women and men do have different psychological makeups, and my approach has to come from being a woman. But I object to making such divisions. I prefer to look at art in terms of good and bad. Just the same, I tend to photograph women and socialize with feminists. When I photograph a woman, I look at her differently from a man. And I also look at a man differently. I think this is based on biology. Sometimes, a photo of mine in a show is not quite right. A man might say of it that it reveals a woman's perspective. This is said as a derogatory remark.

RB: What about family responsibilities?

VB: At times I think that if I were a man, life would be simpler and I'd have fewer responsibilities. Look, an artist is always an artist and creativity is unpredictable. A man does not have to worry about the family or the household. He is busy with his creative process. For me, that is not an option. When I have not prepared a meal, I think about it because I have a daughter. I cannot allow myself the luxury of working full speed. I must always hold something back. Perhaps this defines a woman's approach. Let's say that I have a project in mind that will take all my money. I can't do it because of my responsibilities. I would like more time for my work, but that is also impossible. Sometimes, my daughter takes care of me.

RB: When you look at photographs, can you tell if a woman or a man made it?

VB: Yes, but I cannot explain it. I intuit it. There is a certain energy, or something in it feels close to me, something a man could never do. It's not about themes or styles, but rather about a kind of sensitivity.

RB: When all is said and done, do you feel powerful in your life and in your work?

VB: This is not an easy question. First, we always had equality. You have only to look at the poor women who work at hard labor. There are a million photographs of them. They look fierce with their braids and yellow vests. They built dams and roads. But they are monsters rather than women. A woman should be weaker than a man. It is actually a lot more pleasant when you have next to you a strong man. When you are the only strong one, it is a nightmare, horrible. Yes, I have plenty of energy. But I get tired and depressed periodically, especially in winter. I have an image of myself as a very successful lady who has no problems in life, no inferiority complexes, and for whom all doors are open. People who don't know me can't imagine that I suffer depressions and that I can feel awful and lonely. It is perhaps sinful for me to complain, but I am the only one who knows what is happening inside me.

RB: Bela Matveeva said to me that each of us wears a mask.

VB: Of course I wear a mask. It's a game we play. We have a public face in order to function in the world.

RB: Does being a mother have any connection to your sense of creativity?

VB: A good question. The condition of carrying and bearing a child does have a bearing on my creative process. An idea comes to you and you realize it. It is similar to the experience of giving birth, a physical experience, a sense of completion and of liberation. Having a girl child gives you some kind of wisdom. Bela Matveeva and I work with erotic images. You can do whatever you want with such art—turn it pornographic. But a woman with children will not cross a certain line. There is a limit. Can you take pornographic pictures of your own children? No! Look at these photographs. Here I photographed some gloves that have photographs of lips woven right into them. It's about prostitutes and prostitution. I found these images to be very beautiful. Actually, a real prostitute bought these gloves I made and she wears them on the streets of Berlin. I also did the same kind of thing by sewing photographic images into stockings.

RB: Is this a way of taking back this kind of imagery from men?

VB: Perhaps, but I don't want to think about that. I will say that the images I use are taken from late-nineteenth-century erotic photos of women. The photos are very beautiful.

RB: You use shawls in your work [see fig. 23]. Why?

VB: A shawl covers something. What covers a woman? A man covers a woman. I believe that a man should take care of a woman. He should protect her from all kinds of unpleasantness, to guard and to cherish her. This, I know, is an old-fashioned idea. In my own experience, the men with whom I kept company were always weaker than me, even in terms of sheer energy. When I was about thirty, I finally met a man who could match my energy and who can really help me. He is not at all selfish like a lot of men. I really feel good about having such a friend.

RB: Is he an artist?

VB: He used to be.

Some points Buivid made in her interview were repeated in many others. First, she would like to find a partner who would treat her with respect. Second, life would be easier as a man. A few interviewees even said that in Russian society they would prefer being a man (see Tatiana Faidish interview). Third, when we began to suggest to Buivid and to others that their subject matter might in some way reflect their suppressed anger, they often chose not to respond. And since we would not be there to help pick up the pieces should it have come to that, we chose not to press the issue. Fourth, many believed that they could distinguish between works done by a man or a woman.

Buivid, during a visit to New York in 1998, showed us series of photos of individual nude Russian and American men getting into and splashing around in a bathtub. She said it was easier for the American men to be photographed. We found her project to be very interesting and very different from the cut-up photos sewn into garments. In the latter (which were earlier pieces), the female body parts were decontextualized and de-eroticized because they were simply details and were arranged into patterns that were then absorbed into the overall configurations of the garments. The female body had, in effect, been neutralized. But the entire bodies of the men as they went about their toilette, as it were, were photographed, and therefore they had been turned into objects for the viewer's gaze. Naked and wet, they were entirely vulnerable. These photos mark probably the most complete replacement of the male by the female gaze that we have seen in Russian art. Tania Liberman's photograph of a leg presented as a decorative object, considered in her interview (see fig. 23), parallels Buivid's earlier work. Franceska Kirke's painting of a nude man dancing with a dressed woman, discussed in her interview (see fig. 26), parallels Buivid's bathtub series.

Tania Liberman

Tania Liberman (b. 1964) is a well-known Moscow photographer. Although she says that she explores pornographic imagery, we feel (although we did not argue the point with her) that she deals in surrogate or sublimated pornographic imagery, that as open-minded as she thinks she is, she is still a product of Soviet prudery. One set of works, dating from 1993–1994, shows body parts, especially limbs, with checkerboard grids imposed upon them, thus turning the contours of arms or legs into another kind of design system (fig. 24). The viewer sees the rigid checkerboard of verticals and horizontals yielding to rounded body parts, all transformed into abstract elements interacting with one another. A later series, based on kitchen fixtures, was awash in symbolic phalluses, which were rubber tubes extruded from faucets. In another series, from 1998, Liberman photographed cross-sections of fruits and leafy vegetables, which, because of their crevasses and layered openings, suggest women's genitalia. They also call to mind Georgia O'Keeffe's flower paintings, and as in O'Keeffe's work, Liberman's subjects are objects of the garden or kitchen and not people. Eroticized cross-sectioned cabbages or melons are not pudenda and should never be confused with them. In effect, then, Liberman's photographs titillate, but do not show the real thing. They are, however, beautiful as photographs. This interview was given in 1998.

> **TL:** I was born in Moscow and studied at an ordinary college. It was the only one that taught photography. I left it after three years, in 1985. Since then, I have a rule that I do not work. That is, I work only at my

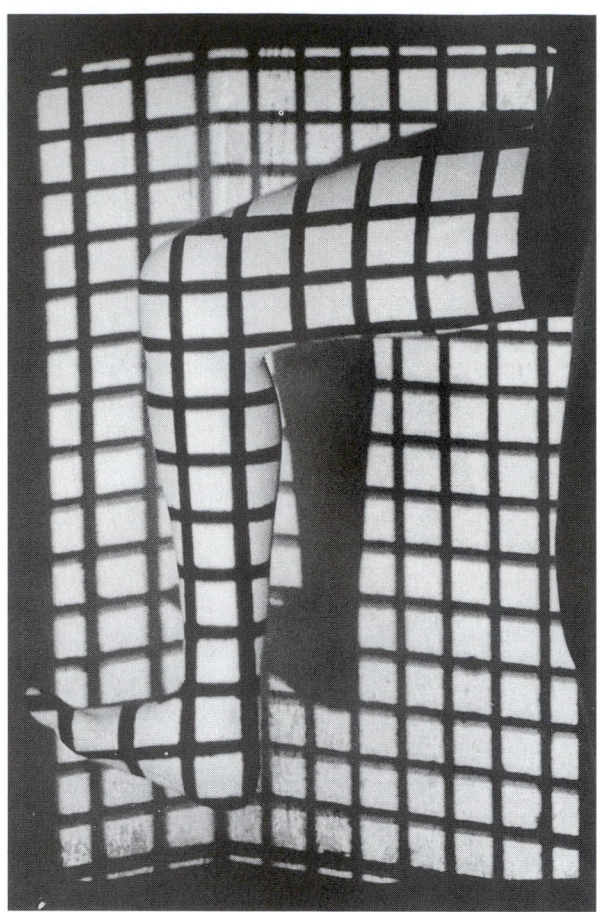

24. Tania Liberman,
Study, 1994, photo-
graph. (Courtesy Tania
Liberman.)
. . . .

photography. My husband works and makes a living, and we have a
child, born in 1991. Actually, my husband is one of the best photographers around, Igor Mukhin. We work in very different ways.

RB: Were your parents supportive?

TL: My father, an aeronautical engineer, was—more so than my mother,
who wanted me to study at the university.

RB: Did you ever feel discrimination?

TL: At the everyday level, yes, but I am a tough person, independent. I
live for today and enjoy my child. My mother never thought about her
child. It is a generational difference. She got married, worked, bore children. It was a banal existence. There is more to life than that. As for
discrimination, I could never go out to a restaurant and have the man
pay for me. I reject that. I consider it an insult and would feel diminished. So I like to pay my own way.

RB: What themes to you explore?

TL: Well, in 1995 I showed the photographs in Kiev of my teapot [especially its spout]. The exhibition was closed immediately as pornographic. Then, for a show in 1996 in Moscow, I based three photos on an old advertisement that was an absolute cliché of male perception of women. Why do men take pictures of women with feathers? It bothered me. This picture was in a book on erotica, which were only begun to be sold in Russia about that time. I noticed that there are definite male clichés in perceiving women. Nothing has changed over the ages. They show women with spread legs or views of their backsides. This was at the XL [Ex El] Gallery where they encourage you to be radical [an interview with the owners is included later].

RB: Are many people exploring issues of pornography in Moscow today?

TL: I think I'm the only one, but others work with erotic themes. But I really manipulate my images. The spout on my teapot, for example, can look like something else.

RB: Are there any feminist organizations in Moscow?

TL: There is a women's union around the president, but it's a club of the wives of officials. There are some small literary groups, but I don't socialize with them. I'm friendly with Natalia Kamenetskaia. We're friends, but we do not discuss feminist questions. As far as I am concerned, this is an entirely private and individual matter. Some people might feel secure or stronger in a group. I'm not looking for anything like that because I feel content with myself. This year [1998] a woman curator wanted some of my works for a women's show. She drove me crazy. I gave her some photos, but I didn't see the show. I don't like exclusive gender associations. A soon as women begin to organize and claim their rights, then they admit to the world that they are weak, that they can't make it on their own. This is how it is in Russia. Earlier, women used to get together to form embroidery clubs to knit and to sew. It's about the same now, except they might paint.

One very important, really overarching, point, mentioned earlier, is that, as Liberman said, women want to become successful on their own, without help, as if they were powerful male artists acting alone. Many women told us that they were held back by men who were in positions of power—as heads of organizations and schools, as jurors, as organizers of exhibitions, and even as purchasers of artworks to be placed in museums. It is an easy step of logic, which the women refuse to take, to realize that the men are not acting as powerful individuals but as part of a patriarchy united, however loosely, to keep women in their place. As the record shows, the men are together on this point. They take care of one another. They network so automatically that nobody is aware that that is what they are doing. Women think that they can succeed without similarly networking. Their model is the lone male who makes it on the basis of his talent. There is, in fact, no such model. It does not happen this way, and the women with whom we spoke resist understanding how the dynamic works.

Maria Snigirevskaia

Maria Snigirevskaia (b. 1965) is a photographer based in St. Petersburg. She photographs many kinds of subjects, but her images of the body place her in proximity to Liberman, or, without an intention to locate her definitively on a particular spectrum, somewhere between Kitaeva and Liberman (see figs. 25, 18, and 24). By using arbitrary lighting techniques, she turns muscular male torsos into abstract forms of light and dark. To a greater extent than Liberman, she allows the body its sense of "bodiness" and therefore its erotic potential. This interview was given in 1998.

> **MS:** I studied photography with Boris Smelov, my stepfather. Unfortunately, he recently died. He taught me at home because there were no schools of photography. Basically, I apprenticed with a master. My mother is Natalia Zhilina, the artist [see interview]. My mother discouraged me from attending art school. She believed schools hindered the creative spirit. My brother, Mitia Shapin [he started the group called Mitki], is also an artist, and he did study at art school. Eventually, I took a job at the Russian State Museum, where I now work.
>
> **RB:** How are you treated there?
>
> **MS:** There used to be more women photographers, but now we are down to two. We had a wonderful woman supervisor, but due to some intrigue, she was let go. Men began to take over and claimed their professional superiority. They are very friendly, but you know things are not right.
>
> **RB:** Do you exhibit very much?
>
> **MS:** I've been in many shows since 1990, even shows in America. My stepfather introduced me to many people. One time, Vita Buivid and I traveled to Sweden, where she curated a photography show. It was an exchange thing with Swedish students. For our Swedish show, Vita and I were the only women in the exhibition. But the Swedes had more

women and only two men. The Swedish women were worried that the Russian men would overpower all of us, so they were extremely aware of any slights. They would not allow the Russian men to help with the suitcases. They were also disturbed when we tried to organize a social evening, especially when one of our guys said to me, "Masha, perhaps you'll take care of things." A woman exploded: "You do it yourself. Masha should not have to do it."

RB: What impression did this make on you?

MS: On the one hand, I liked it, but I think that Swedish women went overboard. I don't see any harm in letting a man carry your suitcase. A woman's constitution is weaker, so why not let a guy do the heavy work?

RB: What do you think the Swedish women were afraid of?

MS: They wanted to show that they were strong, but I didn't see any strength in that. The bigger issue is that women are suppressed in the art world. Men, to express their feelings about women not being capable painters, will say, for example, "Oy, a woman!" *This* upsets me. Not ordinary things like carrying luggage.

RB: So you take issue when it concerns your ability as an artist.

MS: Let me relate an incident. My stepfather was shocked and then, when he told me, I was shocked that when he told a friend that I was having an exhibition, his friend said, "Oy, they allowed a woman?"

RB: Do you participate in women's exhibitions?

MS: My husband does not like such divisions. He believes that when it comes to art, we are all equal. Once I appeared in an all-women's show in Smolensk. I found the all-women show interesting, but it was odd to be only among women. In the branch of the art union to which I belonged, a group of men always thought they were superior. I did not like that, and I do not like separate exhibitions.

RB: How about things at home?

MS: My husband is very good. He is always after me to work, not to become an old hag, a *baba*. He wants me to think less about housework. When I have to be away, he helps, as does my mother. We have an easy relationship.

RB: That is very rare.

MS: My first husband was different. He discouraged me. Every time he saw me buy film, he would mock me.

RB: Your society is very patriarchal. In America, women have been fighting against that.

MS: Our situation is even worse than patriarchal except in very few circles. Before the Revolution, women usually stayed at home. Under the Soviets, women were confused. There was the law of equality, but it really meant that women were harnessed like horses. They worked hard, and when they came home, they worked in the house, cared for the children. It was a double burden. It was disgusting, whereas the men simply went to work and came home. It was a bitter time in our history.

RB: Do you see any changes?

MS: There are some. I see this in discussions with my mother. She had a much harder time. She was constantly reminded that she was a woman and that she could not possibly be taken seriously as an artist. Nobody would dare say such a thing to my face today. Perhaps behind my back, but not to my face. My generation certainly has it better.

RB: Are there women's groups in St. Petersburg?

MS: I don't know. We have a lot of trouble with organizations. We don't have normal clubs where artists can gather. Everybody is in a panic worrying about money.

RB: Tell me about this photograph [fig. 25].

MS: When I look at the body, I see it abstractly—like a sculpture. I focus on the muscles and see them in terms of light and shadow. My work is basically abstract. I like photographing men because I see forms as if they were sculpture.

RB: And women?

MS: I also photograph women, but I like their faces.

RB: I've asked others if they can tell if a work is by a man or by a woman. Some say they can tell.

MS: I never thought about it, but I don't think gender has anything to do with quality. If anybody says they know my work is by a women, then I say they know who I am.

RB: Do you think women are more vulnerable than men?

MS: It is an artificial creation, this powerlessness of women. I think women are stronger. Basically, men sap the energy out of a woman. Without their women, they couldn't accomplish very much. Women are more fit for life. We can cope with difficulties, even in extreme situations like in the Battle of Leningrad during the war. Women coped better. Men died very quickly. Actually, we should find what is strong in each gender and seek to complement each other.

Snigirevskaia's comment about seeing men's bodies in terms of sculpture is interesting in that some women said they had no idea how to paint a man's body and did not find it a very paintable form, anyway. But with a little pushing, they confessed that since their clients were

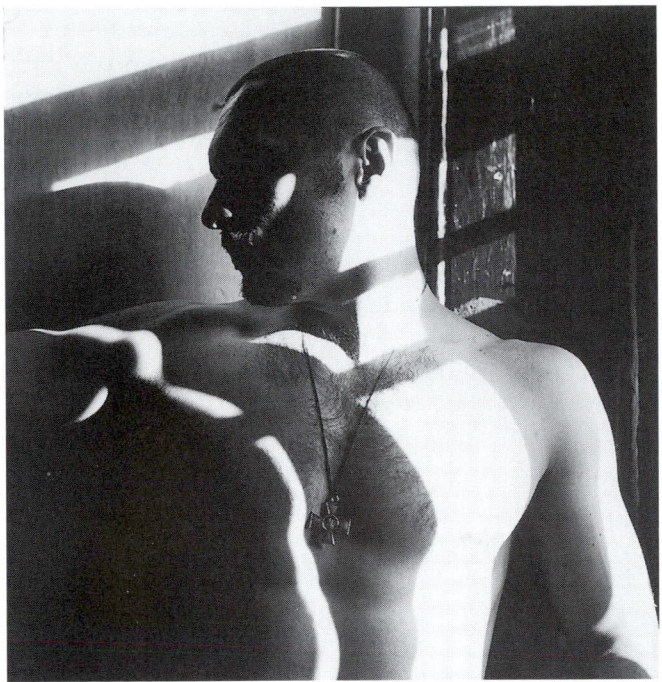

25. Maria Snigirevskaia, *Study*, 1996, photograph. (Courtesy Maria Snigirevskaia.)

usually men, and since men preferred to look at women's bodies, they had to satisfy their client's preferences.

Franceska Kirke

Franceska Kirke (b. 1955), who lives in Riga and graduated from the Latvian Academy of Arts in 1978, was one of those who admitted to painting women or nude women because her male clients preferred them to men. Women's bodies, she said, are softer and more peaceful [here combining visual evidence with social construction]. But, like others, she is not market driven to the exclusion of all other values. On the contrary, her works were among the most complex and sexually transgressive that we were able to see. She explores myth, the art of the past, as well as near-surreal subject matter. For example, she painted a *Rape of Europa* in 1995 with the bull in an expressionist style and the woman in a classical one. The bull, representing animal power, is wounded. So, Kirke asked, "who is the victim?" In another work, *Salome*, three women dance, each holding a head of John the Baptist. This work, she said, was based on lesbians she saw on a street in San Francisco. The women are aggressive and in control of their situation. In the battle of the sexes in this work, women are the winners three times over. In *Impossible Couple* (1992), the man is naked and the woman fully dressed, the reversal of what one might expect from a male artist [fig. 26]. This interview dates basically from 1995, but we have seen Kirke twice since in New York.

RB: Are women and men treated differently in Latvia?

FK: The only difference I can see is that men can devote themselves more fully to their professions than women. I have also heard that men have a better feel for form in art and women for color. I agree with that even though men also work with color. A woman might concentrate more on tones of color, though.

RB: Are there no other differences?

FK: A woman might be less successful because of family obligations. I personally feel like a centaur sometimes. One part of me wants to be a woman—to care for my family, to weed the garden, to be close to the soil. The other half longs to be an artist. The two halves are in perpetual tension. I am unable to drop out, to shut myself off and work. I have to know if my family is safe. I need to have contact with them. Only then can I relax and get down to serious work. A man can easily disappear

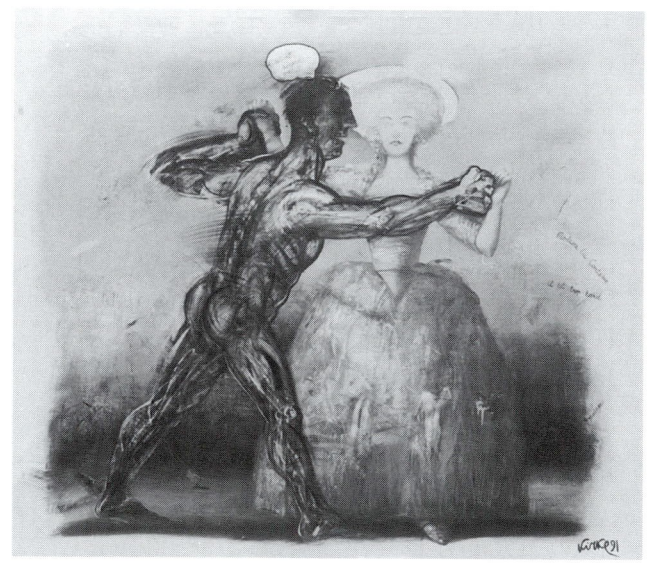

26. Franceska Kirke, *Impossible Couple*, 1992, oil on canvas. (Courtesy Franceska Kirke.)

into his studio for a day or two and nobody will be the wiser. Nobody will wonder where he is. Rather, he will be admired for his seriousness and dedication. But if a woman should do that, she'd be judged harshly. Eyebrows would be raised. People would ask about her children. Yet when a woman does gain professional respect, she becomes a role model for other women. I also think men and women differ in organizational skills. But in terms of craft and technique, there is no difference.

RB: Is there a movement for true equality in Latvia?

FK: Our situation is different from yours. We are more traditional. So it is perfectly natural for a man to assume a leadership position. It is accepted that men are movers, leaders. Men are in privileged positions and we accept that without dwelling on it. We consider it as the way things should be. We think men are well built, tall, and project an impressive, authoritative stance. Very few women in our society are willing to sacrifice everything for a career. Women who do that become global in their development, and then I see no difference between the sexes. A woman might even try a little harder and become more accomplished. Because she is a woman, she might be more diplomatic. She will know better how to get around an issue. But about artists, in our culture, we have always respected artists regardless of gender.

RB: Do you feel different from other Baltic peoples and from the Russians?

FK: We Latvians tend to be different. We are more meditative, introverted, but not passive. Estonians are harder and have close cultural ties with Finland. Lithuanians are more quarrelsome and will never allow anybody to insult them. Estonians are similar, but calmer. We are a peaceful people, and because of that it is difficult for us to stand up to things. We withdraw into ourselves. So I think our art is more lyrical, less concrete, and less related to the specific moment.

RB: What is your background?

FK: My grandfather was an artist, my father a graphic designer, and my mother a costume designer. My daughter is studying painting now. Being an artist is a highly respected profession in Latvia. I went to the art academy here in Riga. There were always more girls than boys in the classes. Girls were more diligent and the boys often got into trouble, but a talented boy would always end up at the academy. You went to the academy usually after studying art in grammar school, high school, and college. Now, you don't need to do all that to become an artist if you have enough energy, knowledge, and self-confidence. But the academy was the only place to train as an artist or a designer. We were usually docile students because we had no other place to go.

RB: What about your teachers?

FK: There were more male teachers, and all the administrators—the chancellor, the dean—were men. There was one woman painting teacher. Some women taught night courses, but I don't think it was due to discrimination (see Malde Muizele's interview). I will not admit to that. Today, our most important curator is a woman.

RB: What about exhibitions?

FK: Quality is the main criterion. Abstractionists, of course, had trouble in the past. I think that style and generational differences caused more problems than gender. Before the Soviets came, we had some wonderful women artists.

RB: Tell me about the male and female images in your work, especially those in the same painting.

FK: I don't paint the struggle between men and women or between European and American cultures. I'm concerned with tensions between high and low art, weak and strong people, different periods in history, surface textures. A man in one of my paintings is a person, a human being who has certain forms. I enjoy painting a woman's body because it is softer and its texture corresponds to peacefulness. I should also say that the clients who buy my pictures are men, and they prefer bodies of nude women. It is generally accepted that a woman should not be muscular. It is the opposite for a man. A male body is interesting for its expression of movement. A man's beauty is in his musculature. A woman has streamlined forms. This is how I look at my pieces, but you see them entirely differently.

RB: In America, for instance, you would rarely see a nude man and a dressed women in the same painting as you have done [see fig. 26].

FK: He represents a certain brutality for me. The two figures also represent two periods in history, a play between his expressionist form and textures and her rococo form and textures. It is a play between classical European art and contemporary expressionism. In my *Rape of Europa,* I am concerned with the relationship of forms. One form, the bull, is animal power, yet he is wounded even though he raped Europa. So who is the victim? This is my own private joke. In the end, he will be turned into parts, with the good parts put into jars of meat.

RB: You have another work that shows a very vulnerable man on a tightrope.

FK: It is not a man, but a person. I wanted to express an idea of a human being and represented it in a man's body. This work dates from 1991 and has political aspects in that the man in the painting is a weak human being squelched by dictators. Men like this one carry on their backs all of society's ills. He carries the weight of history. His existence is very fragile, and at any moment he might fall apart. After I completed it—it was in San Francisco—my foresight came true during the attempted putsch in Russia.

RB: What about your painting of Salome?

FK: There are three women in it. They could be waitresses, since they're carrying something on a plate. It's based on lesbian women I saw in San Francisco, red-dyed hair, aggressive. I turned a classical idea upside down. Usually, the three Graces are represented as delicate women. Here, they are aggressive and suggest that such a situation could exist. In many of my paintings, I leave interpretations open to the viewer. They can go as deep as they want to.

RB: Do you discuss your work with friends?

FK: When we artists get together, we rarely talk about art. I know that in Germany, artists do talk about art. I'm not certain if it is our national characteristic or a generational thing. We do talk to clients, or we used to. Now, the galleries do that for us. I have many clients from Germany.

RB: Is there a feminist movement in Latvia?

FK: Perhaps, but I don't understand what they're about. I have no problems. The whole thing is absurd. If there is a women's movement, then there should be man's movement or a children's movement or a gay movement. We are all equal, and that is the reason why I do not want to participate in such a movement. Actually, I believe that there should never have been equal rights. I am perfectly able to take advantage of my weaknesses. Why should I want to be like a man? That which differentiates me allows me to play the game, and I can even get ahead that way.

RB: How do people see your works?

FK: I have always been happy being invisible, when nobody knows if I am a man or a woman. Most say my works were done by a man. I am not offended by this. Rather, I am proud of the fact that people don't see my work as women's art, but as man's art. But, wait, if I am proud of this, then it means that I consider men to be at a higher level than myself, that they are better artists. This shows that I value men's work more, since I am being taken for a man. Yet I don't want to be treated like a man.

RB: This is complicated to sort out, I know. Let me ask here if your inner voice is based on your experience as a woman.

FK: As an individual, I am not separate from my gender. Yes, my voice comes from my experience. I painted sweet and tender works for a short time after my daughter was born. I was enchanted with my baby. It was so wonderful and sweet, but what I felt was the enchantment of novelty. Gradually, I calmed down and returned to my previous way of thinking.

Kirke touched on several issues that others had mentioned to a greater or lesser extent. First, the criteria for quality in art have been so gendered that she cannot disentangle them from those applied to art done by men. As much as she and others say that good art is good art and bad art is bad art, they also say that, since they want to be thought of as male artists, then good, or at least better, art is art done by men. She enjoys the thought that her art has been mistaken for a man's, but at the same time it forces her to admit that women's art is inferior. Second, she wants to be independent, but will resort to feminine wiles to get her way. Third, she is opposed to a feminist movement, which might give her a certain kind of strength, in order to take advantage of her weaknesses as a woman. Fourth, having a child, or, more precisely, giving birth had a profound, if temporary, effect on her work. Whether stated implicitly or explicitly, giving birth, the ultimate female experience, is somehow threatened by the feminist movement, which somehow defeminizes women. Feminism does not allow them to be women as eastern Europeans understand what it means to be a woman (seemingly fragile, etc.), and perhaps, in their heart of hearts, they want to be fragile. The feminist movement, in effect, is seen as another kind of oppression rather than as a tool to achieve a better life. Or, to say it differently, liberation is too scary to contemplate.

To elaborate further about the fourth point, giving birth is also a very private act, and because of that it had political implications under Soviet rule. It assumed and still assumes an importance that we feel is not entirely understood in the West. To explain better what kind of thinking is involved here, we want to place next the interview with Alla Mitrofanova, a St. Petersburg–based art critic and art historian.

Alla Mitrofanova

Alla Mitrofanova (b. 1960) was very pregnant when we interviewed her in 1995.

> **AM:** I see my pregnancy as a very interesting experience. It is my individual experience—spiritual, psychological, physiological. I am ob-

serving and studying myself. I know it sounds rather funny, but I am observing the pregnancy in a historicocultural context. I am thirty-five years old. I could have given birth a lot earlier, in the 1980s. I chose not to. When the country fell apart after perestroika, I found myself in a dangerous position. Anything was possible. I felt alone in a kind of spiritual isolation because suddenly there was no single social or cultural structure for support any longer. To cope with my sense of spiritual isolation, I needed the experience of my body. I decided to embark on a radical experiment—to become pregnant. I now understand life in a special way. I know that it is possible to live outside the political and cultural chaos all around me. What I mean is that self-awareness during the 1970s was tied to structural social models. This gave a feeling of security even if you were in opposition to the state. At that time, I was not an individual. My body did not rightfully belong to me. It belonged to medicine, to the state. Now, my pregnancy gives me the opportunity to make my body my own in our new situation. And because of that, my body requires its own theory.

In the blink of an eye, what might be considered a renegotiation of the essentialist nature of women, by the simple act of taking control of one's own body, became a radical attack on Soviet genderless policies, on its intrusiveness into the lives of people, and on the fear people felt after the fall of Communism. A seriously complicating factor is the memory of the old Soviet line of propaganda to the effect that having babies makes a woman a heroine of the state. So Mitrofanova treated her pregnancy as a cultural rather than a biological event. Her organs of childbearing were now hers and could become part of her reinvention of herself as an individual. They became, in effect, central to a new cultural construction of identity and of the nature of personal choice. In her own mind, this experience would be crucial to an understanding of the fact that she finally owned her own body. For Mitrofanova, the primal act of creation became the essential act of asserting her own individuality—her body, her choice, her pregnancy, her baby. It indicates the kind of half-crazed life people led before the collapse of Communism—Soviet on the outside, personal on the inside, psychologically paralyzed in both ways—and the dread they felt in the years immediately after. No wonder women such as Franceske Kirke (see previous interview) want to cling to what is intrinsically theirs—their femininity.

Awareness of one's own femininity, however, is not just about having babies. It begins, no doubt, in childhood, and for many it became an issue in art school. In the following three interviews, Natalia Turnova, Zoya Frolova, and Elena Korennova discuss their schooling, in addition to other matters.

Natalia Turnova

Natalia Turnova (b. 1957) paints large, cartoonlike heads, but there is nothing cartoon-like in her intentions (fig. 27). Her interview is interesting for the information she gives concerning art school training and exhibiting her work. Although she did not reveal to us the same kind of anger as Zvezdochetova, she nevertheless described similar experiences.

27. Natalia Turnova, *Lenin Playing Chess,* 1990, oil on canvas. (Courtesy Natalia Turnova.)

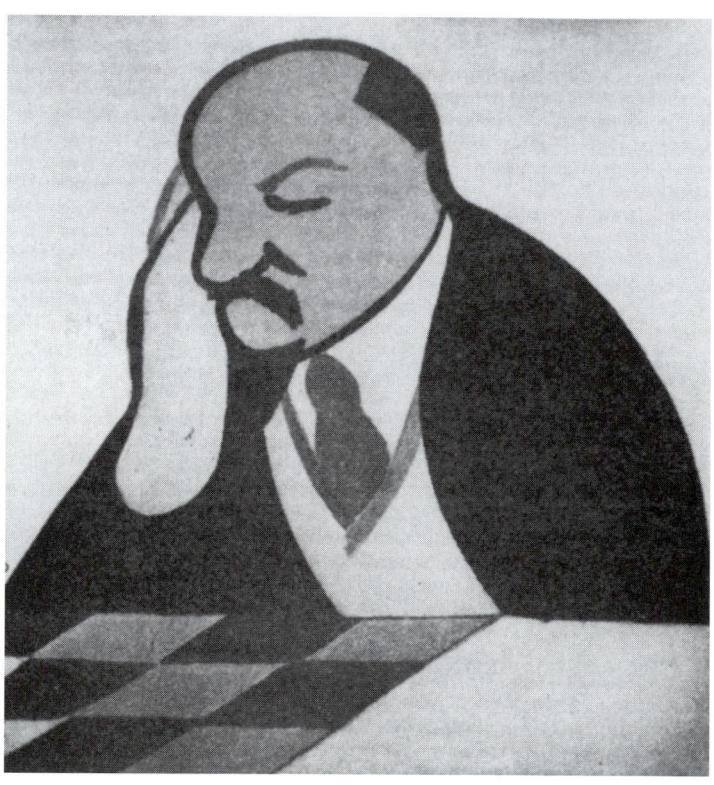

RB: What themes interest you?

NT: I have a child and I decided to make a portrait series. They grow up so fast that I wanted to do a series.

RB: Do you think male artists would do the same?

NT: I know only one, Dima Vrubel, who paints family scenes.

RB: What about your education?

NT: I studied design in the commercial art section here in Moscow at the Stroganov Art Institute and graduated in 1983. But I realized that there was not much future for a designer here, so I began to paint. There was a place, the Malaya Gruzinskaia Exhibition Hall, where you could occasionally show some abstract works, but for one evening only. These showings were organized by the sculpture section of the artists' union when things had eased up a bit. But of course now all of that no longer matters.

RB: What was the Stroganov like?

NT: There were fewer women there, except in the weaving and ceramics departments. In the design department, we were four women and seven men. It was difficult for women to get into the art department and practically impossible to get into the sculpture department. Most of the teachers were men. There was a woman art historian, and a few women taught drawing.

RB: What kind of attention did you get?

NT: It depended on what kind of a student you were. Serious students were given the most attention. But one teacher repeatedly told us that we women should not bother studying because we would get married and forget our education. But I felt no discrimination.

RB: Who encouraged you to study art?

NT: I was lucky to have a wonderful mother. In our country, higher education is revered. If you go to college, you gain respect, and it is, or was, assumed that you would be taken care of for life. So my mother encouraged me to get a higher education even though she was near retirement age and had very little money. I moved in with her because I could not afford to live on my own. The important thing was the psychological rather than the financial support. She always stood by me. Even when I had a child, she helped me take care of him.

RB: And your father?

NT: My parents divorced when I was eighteen. My mother took care of my two sisters and me.

RB: How did you get into exhibitions?

NT: The organizers were men. At the place where I could show, they were usually Boris Orlov, Pasha Malinovski, and Dimitri Prigov. Maybe about 20 percent of the artists in the shows were women. In general the interesting artists in Moscow are men. They picked people they know. Sometimes, there were so many, they could pick only those whom they knew. I was not invited to some shows because I had no affiliations or close contacts, although we all knew each other. Had I been a man, it would have been simpler. I would have met them, sat around, had a couple of drinks, and we would bond. As a woman, this was a closed situation. The same was true for getting studio space from the union. For a very long time, I could not get one, and it was enormously expensive to rent one. To get one, you had to know somebody, become a close friend, drink together. For a woman, this was, again, problematic. Our entire system works on private relationships, and this is difficult for a woman.

RB: What about equal rights?

NT: We had equality of duty, but not of rights. All of that was just slogans that had nothing to do with real life. It's hard for a woman to lift heavy canvases and bring large paintings to shows. Nobody helps. The understanding was that if you made large works, you brought them yourself. Otherwise, you needn't bother. What this meant was that you shouldn't push yourself where you don't belong. This was how many women were eliminated from exhibitions. That and taking care of the household. It put us on a secondary level.

RB: Did you have enough time to work?

NT: Before I had a child, I certainly had enough time, but not after. I did not exhibit for about three years. I had little help except from my mother and my husband, who recently died. He was an art photographer. We helped each other. I was lucky to be married to him. He understood that I was an artist and that my work was important to me. It didn't matter who prepared dinner. He learned how to take care of himself and had no hang-ups about going shopping, washing dishes, that sort of thing. I know artist couples where the husband believes he comes first. We did not have such a relationship. Nevertheless, he spent much less time caring for the baby, and he also had a sense of entitlement, particularly when he had to choose between family and work. If the baby got sick, I was the caregiver. This was quite natural. We never even discussed this. Even when the child was healthy, I was the caregiver. And even though I earned more money than he, he still felt that he was the one who earned the family income. Yet he deferred to me as the better artist.

RB: What was it like with your parents?

NT: They were entirely different. My father would sit at the table and wouldn't get up to take care of anything for himself. He would yell at my mother for a glass of water. She was a teacher and worked very hard. She brought student assignments home, but my father's behavior was normal. All Russian men behaved this way. When he came home, *he* was tired. *He* worked, but he did not consider my mother in the same light. As soon as a man begins to earn a living and makes more than his wife, he assumes the role of a patriarch.

RB: How is the situation now?

NT: I would never go back to the way things were, but they are harder now. On the other hand, I might have felt internally free before, but had no way to express that sense of freedom. Now, I need no approval. Then, we had a system of inner control imposed from without, a censoring mechanism that told you how to behave in the eyes of others. All of this was very powerful. So oppression was not based just on gender.

RB: Even so, what changes do you feel?

NT: I got involved in a small women's exhibition in the mid-1990s. This was good, but just the same, a woman artist has to be better than a man in order to get attention. A male artist always comes before a woman artist. He occupies first place and the woman is always second. In order to strike a balance, you have to work much harder. I know this because there are many mediocre male artists who live very comfortably and who can exhibit in many places. A woman in similar circumstances would not be noticed at all. Nobody would bother with her. But men have connections. It's all a boys club that women cannot crash. The men look out for one another. A woman named Larissa Pashuk often organizes shows. A while ago, she held an exhibition titled *The Russian Feminist* to which she invited ten women. On opening day, a male artist had a show in the same gallery that opened an hour later. Nobody came to Pashuk's opening despite invitations, but the man's opening was packed. Nobody wants to go to a woman's show. The word *feminist* has a negative connotation here. Women's art is a minus in the context of the Moscow art scene.

RB: What about feminist groups?

NT: I don't know of any such group, but I am friendly with Natalia Kamenetskaia. Everybody knows her. As for me, artists see me as a person, and friends treat me with respect. They know that a woman artist is more important than a male because they understand our predicament. But such people are both rare and highly intelligent. Let me tell you a story. In the early 1990s, Natalia organized a feminist exhibition that included my work. I mentioned this to my sister, who is very well educated. She replied in horror, "Why are you joining the feminists?" I told her that I was not joining them, but that I was just exhibiting with Natalia. My sister said that men would not like that, that feminism carries a stigma, that it is connected with homosexuality. You can see the negative image it projects. (This is still apparent in 2000.)

RB: Does your apprehension of reality depend on your experiences as a woman?

NT: I would have to say yes. My domestic activities do penetrate my consciousness and my work. The paintings I made of political leaders were transgressive and broke with stereotypical representations of these people [see fig. 27]. I am not interested in these men, per se, but in breaking the mold, destroying the clichés with which they are represented. I select well-known personalities so that the viewer will get my point of view. I show them playing games, that sort of thing.

RB: I see that you made paintings of your husband during his illness.

NT: When my husband became ill, I made a series of paintings of him. I wanted to express how I felt. I wanted to convey the meaning of what was happening in my life, that maybe it might interest others. My husband's illness was real and it was part of my experience. Would a man do the same if he had to care for a sick spouse or child? I don't know, but it's easier for men to distance themselves from such situations, to become abstracted.

RB: Do you think women are more vulnerable?

NT: Generally speaking, yes. A woman has to be vulnerable, otherwise she is considered aggressive and very unpleasant even to other women. On the other hand, a woman has to defend herself and remain feminine at the same time. It's difficult. You lose something when you are tough. Your male friends value your strength, especially in your art, because they don't want a partner who is weak. Yet, at the same time, they want a women to remain soft. A woman is supposed to hide her strength, like a cat that hides its claws. An aggressive woman alienates everybody.

RB: What about male aggressiveness?

NT: I don't like that quality in men or women, but it's more natural for men. Women are not supposed to have such feelings.

RB: Can you tell if a painting is by a man or a woman?

NT: I hardly think so. A weak painting is a weak painting. But many judge a weak painting to be by a woman.

RB: What about your recent work?

NT: They deal with automobiles. To be a woman behind the wheel in Moscow is a terrifying experience. Women are not regarded as people. Men yell and keep a distance. I don't know how driving is in the West.

RB: It's like breathing.

The anecdotes Turnova told about her father, her husband, her art teacher, finding exhibition space, feminism, and getting along with people were repeated in one form or another by virtually every interviewee.

Ieva Iltnere

Ieva Iltnere (b. 1957) graduated from the Latvian Academy of Arts in 1982. She explores in her work the domestic sphere—such as children's parties—and images of women. This interview was given in 1996.

II: In Latvia, women are not usually involved in politics, but there are very many involved in the arts. My father is an artist and my mother designs textiles. She also raised the children. This was not an issue. My father did not want me to paint. He said that it is a difficult profession for a woman—a woman and art, a woman and a family—that it would take everything out of me. I felt sorry for my mother. She had talent, but no time to make art. She had no choice in the matter. I think now it gives her pleasure that I paint, that I could find some balance between my family and my work. She's happy that I am not a Sunday painter, but a serious professional. At first, I had decided to go to a school of applied arts. I studied ceramics, and my parents thought that at least I could earn a living making pots.

RB: In other words, a woman's occupation.

II: Yes, but my father was in general dissatisfied with me. He is very patriarchal and was used to making the decisions. I had decided to study decorative arts. Then I went to the academy.

RB: How was the academy?

II: Before I went there, the majority of my teachers were women. At the academy, they were men. It is a male bastion, even though some of our art galleries are run by women. We were about half boys and half girls at the academy. There was no distinction in the way we were treated. After I finished, I taught at a vocational school. I know that the selections committee selected more boys than girls. At first they would look at the works, and then ask which ones were painted by boys. They chose the boys first. Perhaps there were not enough boys in the school. I say this because there are so many women artists in Latvia.

RB: But was there equality?

II: Of course, there was no total equality, but life is not equal. In art exhibitions, it didn't matter if the artist was a man or a woman. This was not an issue for us. The family situation was different. It was clear the role women were supposed to play. A man had an existence entirely different from a woman. A woman stayed at home and took care of the children. Now, we also have careers.

RB: Have you ever felt discrimination?

II: Your question touches me personally. Lately, artists have been making large pieces and installations. These require a lot of energy and physical strength, and if I make one, it takes all my time. Here, I am at a disadvantage as a woman, because I also have to make supper for my family and do house chores. At these times, I envy my husband, who can leave in the morning for the day, go to his studio, where he can be occupied with his own work, make some phone calls. I don't have the same privileges as he does. I have to be home for the children at a certain time and do things with and for them. All these obligations are stifling, and I feel my brain is cut into different pieces and placed in different compartments. But my husband can allow his project to take up his entire mind. I become envious when this happens and experience myself as weak. I have no strength left. On the other hand, I know that being a painter is the only way possible for me. So I have learned to budget my time in order to paint one or two hours a day in my studio. And when I'm not there, my mind is still occupied with ideas and visual images. When I have a show, I spend much more time in my studio. I do only what is absolutely necessary at home. My family knows to leave me alone at those times or to pitch in and help in the kitchen. Then, I can be very productive. One of my sons likes to cook and my husband will help out with the heavier work—male-type things—but he doesn't like detail or rote work. But they help, otherwise I would go under. Also, there is no end to house work, but a painting is different. It is permanent and lasting, whereas laundry is constant and continuous. I have to paint to preserve something for myself.

RB: Do you have friends for support?

II: Dzemma Skulme [see interview] was an inspiration to all of us.

RB: I mean personal friends?

II: There is some organization in Riga, but I am not involved. I don't think women artists are involved in any way.

RB: What about your images?

II: I think you can tell immediately that they were done by a woman

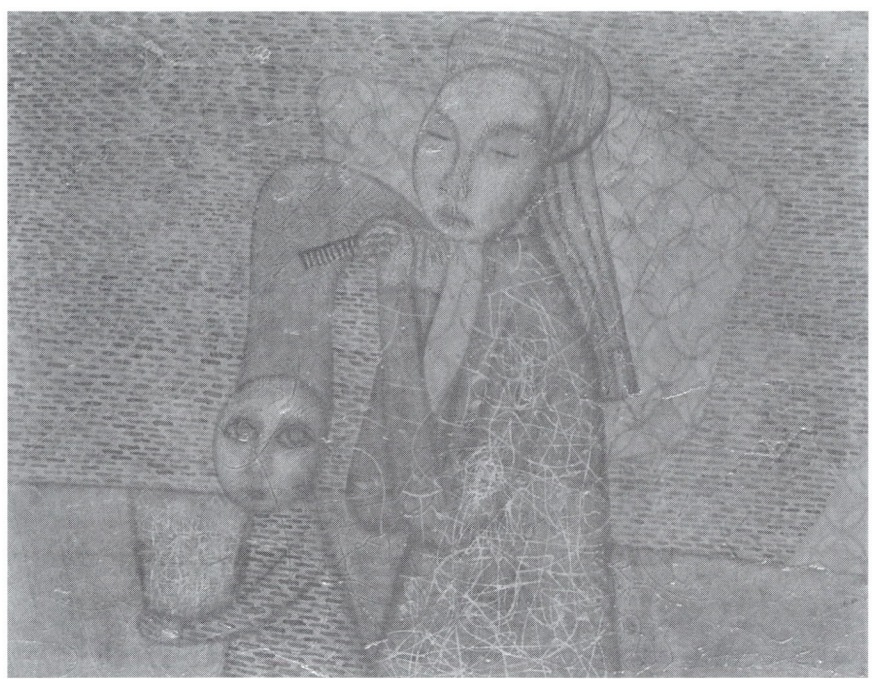

28.   Ieva Iltnere, *Red Room*, 1995, oil on canvas. (Courtesy Mimi Ferzt Gallery, New York.)

[fig. 28]. I like to paint women and children because they do not express brutality. I seldom portray men in my pictures. Perhaps it has something to do with my own identity. Perhaps I seek a reflection of myself. Men require a different approach, a cubist or an expressionist one. I would need a different format, a larger one. I sometimes paint two women in a picture because it suggests a feeling of community. Perhaps it is because I have two sisters. I also like to paint mothers and children. It's not so much the theme that interests me as the formal interest I take in large and small forms. But I also think that women are more emotional in their approach to art than men.

Iltnere was one of the few who commented on selection processes at schools. All the interviewees discussed their own schooling, and their responses ranged from either not remembering or not experiencing any discrimination as students to complaints about discrimination, especially in the higher grades. Evidently, it depended on the teachers rather than the school, city, or country. Virtually all said that women teachers usually handled the lower grades whereas men were in charge of the upper grades, and that women taught the collateral courses (history, philosophy), while men led the art classes. Elena Keller (see following interview) was quite explicit about some of her memories as a student as well as a young artist seeking exhibition spaces.

Elena Keller

Elena Keller (b. 1951), an abstract artist, was born in Moscow and now lives in the New York area. Although her work is quite removed from feminist concerns, her experiences provide us with some insight into the lives of young women artists in the 1970s and 1980s. This interview was given in 1996.

EK: I went to the In Memory of 1905 Art School. The preparation was the traditional kind. We were about thirty at the start, evenly divided between boys and girls, and at the end we were much fewer, with the boys outnumbering the girls at least three to one. I remember girls being treated in a condescending way because not much was expected of them. Whatever I achieved was through my own stubbornness and constant hard work. Most of the male teachers, though, did spend a lot of time with the girl students. They would stand behind the girls and put their hands on the girls' shoulders and caress them. The girls were seen as beautiful objects. The prettier the girl, the more she commanded attention. Talent was not a consideration here.

RB: What about you?

EK: I had a sense that my teachers noticed my merits and qualities. I sensed that they had respect for me. From my group, I am the only woman who is still an artist. Others went into the applied arts.

RB: What about exhibitions?

EK: There was a newspaper called *The Moscow Artist* that provided information on shows. There were always fewer women on the juries. Men would say, "What kind of shows are we having? There are nothing but women." They limited the number of women in shows—not necessarily out of spite, but because that was their mentality. They preferred to give places to men. Perhaps they felt that women could not reach a high enough intellectual level, and that their place was in the kitchen. I don't know what they thought, but men always predominated. When I would be pushed aside, I didn't get mad or upset. I just got more stubborn. There was nothing overt. That was just the system.

RB: What about women jurors?

EK: Well, divas don't want competition. It was impossible to fight it. Even after perestroika, nothing changed. Let me tell you, I tried not to be too visible physically. My last name, Keller, does not have a feminine ending, so many men assumed I was a man. Perhaps nobody would think that my work was done by a woman. The director of the State Tretiakov Gallery bought one of my paintings and did not know I was a woman.

RB: Were there women with whom you could commiserate?

EK: No. Everybody accepted the conditions and didn't complain. You got used to them. Even during Gorbachev's time when there was terrible inflation, you would think that people would complain. No. They were frightened and tried to save what they could, but nobody raised questions. Russians are not used to standing up for their rights or opposing the state. They are brought up to obey and to be submissive to their fate. But among artists, we could at least experience our inner freedom and dare to develop in our own way.

RB: Was this easier after the fall of the Soviet Union?

EK: During perestroika, a group of women decided to organize a show. We included a male sculptor only because we needed some physical help hanging our paintings. The rest of us understood one another's work and one another's ambitions. The show was an act of affirmation for us. We did not exhibit as women artists, but as artists. It was very easy for us to get along without men. We agreed on issues, and we knew that if we invited one male painter, he would manipulate us into inviting some of his friends.

RB: In your abstract paintings, do you find a female voice?

EK: I can't say, but I think as a woman I am endowed with some special feeling of harmony, something innate in the way of gracefulness and refinement.

Tatiana Hengstler, a Moscow-based artist who spends time in European cities and in New York, recounted some unpleasant stories about exhibitions. In a joint exhibition with a man, her name would appear second. On one occasion, an artist wrote a note saying that the participation of a woman artist was unusual. Hengstler said that he might just as well have written the word *monkey* as *woman*. She also made the important point, which was reiterated time after time, that the wives of male artists are secretaries, helpers, and gofers, but nobody helps a woman artist.

Zoya Frolova

Zoya Frolova (b. 1954), who graduated from the Kharkov Art Institute in 1976, is Ukrainian, married to a Latvian artist, identifies as Russian, immigrated to the United States in 1995, and lives in Jersey City, New Jersey. Her style is soft-focus representational and her subject matter is very allusive. It might include clownlike figures and nudes whose attitudes and postures defy gravity and specific meaning (fig. 29). This interview began in 1995 and has been continued at many get-togethers since then.

RB: How did you begin to study art?

ZF: My father registered me in art school. He had wanted to be a painter, but the war prevented him from studying art. I studied in Kharkov, first in a children's art school, and then I took preparatory courses for the art institute there. I skipped the art high school, which was not

2 9. Zoya Frolova, *The Three Graces*, 1996, oil on canvas. (Courtesy Zoya Frolova.)

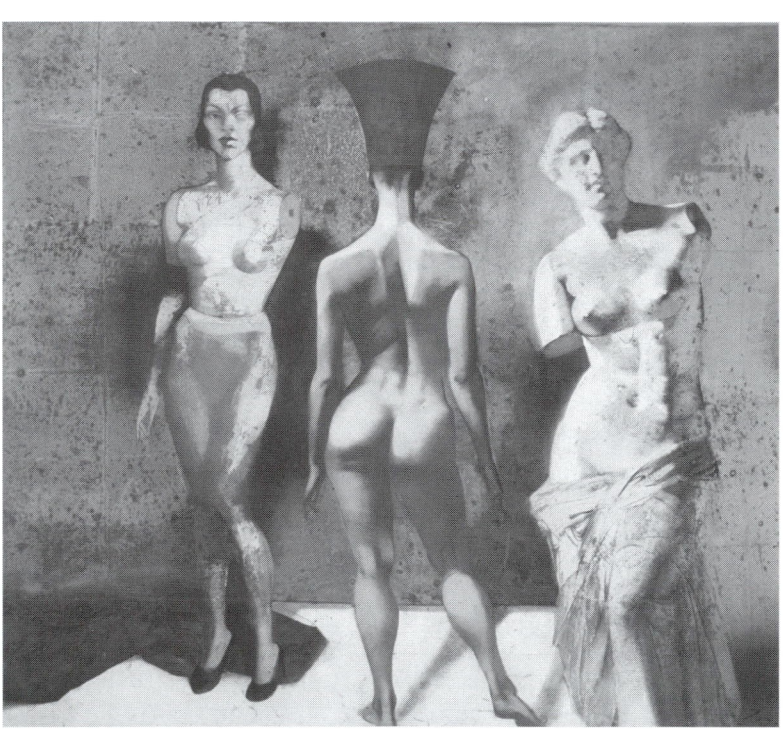

compulsory. I had talent, but there was no star system. It was hard work. Kharkov, not Kiev, was the cultural capital of Ukraine, but it was ultimately restrictive and provincial. Even though I had a teacher who was part of the first avant-garde of the 1920s, I liked classical art the best. Because we were so far away from everything, we traveled to Moscow and Leningrad twice a year to see exhibitions. I tried to absorb everything like a sponge.

RB: Were there many women in your courses?

ZF: Half the students were women. But in my program on monumental art [mural painting, large-scale easel painting], there were very few. It required a great deal of physical strength and a lot of money. The authorities thought there was no reason to spend funds on women who would probably never become professional artists. Our education was free, but funds were limited. To get into the program, you had to be ten times better than a man so that they could not avoid admitting you. Officially, nothing was said, but that's how it worked. The teachers could tell who was capable and who might last through the program. Officially, all were equal, but in reality it was different. It took a year of class work before you could apply, and then you had to submit a completed project.

RB: What about exhibitions?

ZF: They never asked about gender. If your work was good, the officials selected it.

RB: Did women explore feminine themes?

ZF: No. I had no problems, nothing to fight for. That is why I did not and do not focus on specific women's themes. I paint images of women because I find a woman's body to be more expressive. There is more contrast and it gives the impression of greater vulnerability. In my work, I want to express something about the human condition that should be accessible to everybody, everywhere.

RB: Where does your inspiration come from?

ZF: My most powerful impulses come from anger, from situations I cannot change and have no power over. For example, I remember seeing soldiers open fire on a peaceful group of people in Tbilisi, Georgia, who wanted independence for their country. I made a painting called *The General* after that. My husband [the artist Janis Jacobson] thinks women are more sensitive than men and experience life and human relations at a very intense level. This could be a hindrance because we lose distance, but I try to keep that in mind. He thinks men are more rational and intellectual. I know that women are also rational, but we have an emotional side. That's why we react so differently from men, more spontaneously and impulsively. We each have our place in the world. For men, it is at war, for women, in the hospitals.

RB: What about organizations?

ZF: Women are too busy. We are so overloaded that we have no time to join organizations. Everything at home is her responsibility, plus a job. When I see a woman from a political organization, I see a person who is a tough babe.

RB: What do you think about equal rights?

ZF: After all those laws were passed, nobody bothered to think about them. Women understood one thing—they had no time to take advantage of their rights, but they knew they had them. Women are still struggling for basic needs. In medical clinics, for example, where 98 percent of the doctors are women, the director will be a man. It's the same story in the schools.

RB: What about family life?

ZF: My husband is very helpful—cooks, does the laundry, and is good at housework. As artists, we understand and respect each other.

Elena Korennova

Elena Korennova (b. 1960) paints in a meticulously detailed mannerist-rococo style. People in her works are often in elegant costumes. Flowers and ornaments are precisely rendered (fig. 30). From Moscow, Korennova immigrated to the United States in the early 1990s and currently resides in New York. This interview began in 1995 and continues to this day.

RB: Was there much competition in art school?

EK: Teachers would single out and support one person. This created conflict. But generally, competition was fair and friendly. At the Stroganov Art Institute, there were more women teachers and fewer girl students because only one-third of the class could be girls. The reason is that everybody expected the girls to drop out. It really happened that way. But teachers would give girls low grades, anyway.

RB: What about getting accepted?

EK: Applicants were supposed to submit drawings without last names attached to them. But some students were admitted through bribery. That means somebody knew the names. I would say that about half the students came in that way.

RB: Can you tell if a work is made by a man or a woman?

EK: Student work tends to be similar. Everybody draws from the same

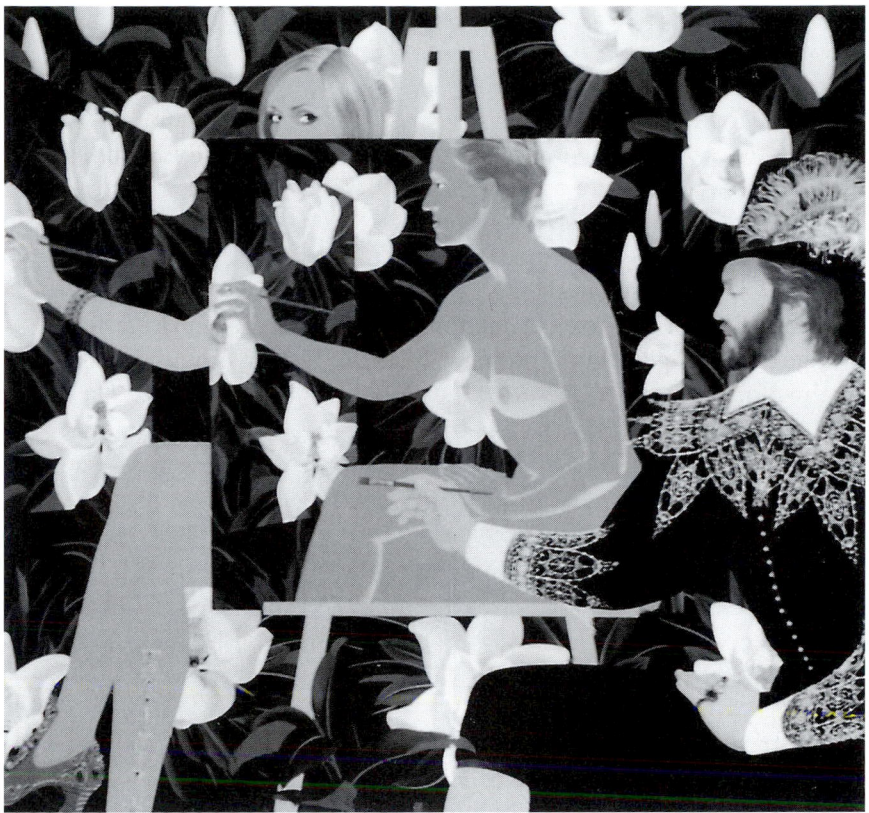

30. Elena Korennova, *One More Time about Love,* 1994, acrylic on canvas. (Courtesy Elena Korennova.)

models. Later, women will develop a distinct style. They are drawn to beauty, although each has her own concept of beauty. This does not work so well with the older artists who were not allowed to develop feminine themes. It was considered a weakness if a work showed any feminine qualities. It would be labeled "women's art." It meant that the artist was a *khudoznitsa,* a woman artist or a craftsperson, not a *khudoznik,* an artist. The female ending always has a pejorative connotation. A man or a woman must always be a *khudoznik.* That's why every woman wants to show that she is a strong and powerful artist, that she can be as manly as a man. She does not want anybody to suspect that the work is done by a woman, but rather by a genderless artist.

RB: What inspires you?

EK: I am a realist, but I also fantasize especially when I try to make life a little better than it is in actuality. This is a purely feminine trait. Look at my work. Nobody would ever confuse it with a man's work. My paintings are absolutely feminine. When I lived in Russia, I tried to suppress my feminine leanings because I knew it was wise to do so. When I arrived in America, I stopped feeling embarrassed about my feminine tendencies. In Russia, I knew that I should not paint anything beautiful. If you paint a self-portrait, you should not wear a pretty dress. Also, you should alter your facial features so as not to appear pretty. I remember being told not to paint myself too attractively. Tatiana Nazarenko [see interview], who is a beautiful woman, painted herself almost in caricature.

RB: What about men?

EK: Men can do as they please. But in Soviet times, their pictures could not be sentimentalized. The union would object. Somebody would tell them that everything was fine, but that something needed fixing. All of this was done with a good spirit.

RB: What about the work of other women?

EK: I think I can see in the style and theme that a work is by a woman. Not in every case. I don't think it's an honor to be confused with a man. The works of our best women artists, especially those from Latvia, can be seen to have been done by women. I find their works far superior to those of men. No man can dispute that.

RB: Was there networking when you were in art school?

EK: No. I did not participate in women's shows, because the quality was pretty weak. For the union shows, women who did not exhibit with the men were given their own space, but their work also tended to be weak. If a special women's show was held, the message was, "Shut up, you are getting your show! Stop complaining!" This sort of thing was done pro forma.

RB: What happened after perestroika?

EK: Everything fell apart, especially for high school students. All textbooks were now filled with misinformation that once had been truth. Everybody was terribly confused and had no idea of what was coming next. In art, suddenly there was artistic freedom. Some clown could call himself an artist and expose his penis in the Arbat [a Greenwich Village–type street], call it a happening or a performance, and then try to get a foundation to subsidize him.

RB: Have you ever felt discrimination?

EK: Not really. I know it exists, and I might even have been excluded from exhibitions because I am a woman. Since I am not a feminist and don't struggle for my rights, I don't always notice the slights. True, when

I first wanted to leave for America, I did experience something like discrimination. I was not allowed to leave. For an exhibition that was to take place in America at the time, the American hosts saved one-quarter of the spaces for women. Not one women was allowed to leave Russia—this was 1989. The authorities sent KGB agents instead. We told our American friends, who then opened up two more spaces for women, for particular women. I was one of the two. Still, the authorities sent men. The Americans were really upset. Sasha, my husband [the artist Alexander Petrov], could have gone, but remained with me. Another couple had a similar story. Even though they both signed the paintings as if they were joint products, it was the wife who did all the work. Nobody was supposed to know, and since she was promoting his career, she was happy when he went even though she had to stay behind. Discrimination is odd in Russia. There are more female than male teachers. It's considered a women's occupation. The same with doctors. But what does a woman doctor do? She works like a horse in some clinic. She has to make rounds, maybe thirty patients a day in her district. This means walking because she has no car, walking from apartment house to apartment house, up the steps to the fifth floor, and so on. Then, when she gets home, she has to prepare the evening meal while her husband is sprawled out on the couch. After that, she has to do the dishes while he reads the newspaper or watches TV. She cannot really build a career like a male doctor. A man can rise in the medical profession, become a professor, a surgeon, earn a lot of money. A woman doctor is like a horse dragging a heavy load. It's the same for women engineers. There are very few women at the supervisory level.

RB: Why do women marry so young in Russia?

EK: There is no living space. There is no place to make love in private. Young people do not live together as in America. A young man in Russia might share a room with his parents and siblings. In Russia, you have sex publicly—on the street, at the beach, in the bushes. Eventually, the couple gets married and lives in tiny rooms with their parents. The high divorce rate is due to lack of space and oppressive in-laws, especially the boy's mother, who is the boss of the apartment. There is an enormous number of battered wives because everybody is frustrated.

RB: Are boys and girls raised differently in Russia?

EK: Girls are not encouraged to cry or to be overly emotional, but people will say to a boy, "Why do you cry like a girl?" I have my feminine side, but also a masculine one. People think I'm a guy in skirts. But in the house, Sasha is the boss. Just the same, you have to be tough. Show the slightest bit of weakness and you will be eaten up. When we lived in

Italy before coming to the United States, a gallery owner wanted our works at no cost to himself. He told me that he never met such an iron-clad woman, that I was a regular Margaret Thatcher. Of course, he didn't know that I would fall apart every night when I got home.

Korennova raised an issue that we heard a few times—whether the husband or the wife takes credit for a joint work. This issue relates to others, such as who speaks for the couple and whose career is emphasized perhaps at the expense of the other's. Vera Khlebnikova has, among other comments, a few words on the subject. After her interview, we will look at some interviews in which the couples work as a team and in which the husband, even if he is not an artist, insists on speaking for his wife.

Vera Khlebnikova

Vera Khlebnikova (b. 1954) is heir on both sides of her family to generations of distinguished artists. It is a responsibility she carries with her in her life and in her work. She was also the partner of Andrei Monastirski, when in 1976 in Moscow he founded the Collective Actions group, a loose organization involved with rituals, performances, and group participation activities. In recent years, she has made collages composed primarily of documents, letters, and various papers taken from family archives in her possession.

> **VK:** My name is Vera Khlebnikova, but officially my last name is Miturich-Khlebnikova. My grandfather, Piotr Vasilevich Miturich [1887–1956], and my father, Mai, were both artists. To avoid confusion, I began to sign my work "Khlebnikova." My maternal grandmother's name was also Vera Khlebnikova. She was a Sunday painter and died in 1940. Her brother was Velímir Khlebnikov, the poet and mystic.
>
> **RB:** Tell me about your work with Andrei Monastirski.
>
> **VK:** He was the leader of Collective Actions and I was in the first performance. With this piece and with others, we talked things out. I was the devil's advocate. Sometimes, I came up with ideas for performances—particularly the ones called *Spherical Object, Slogan, Rape,* and *Scissors.* For this last one, which was about 1978, we wrote "Hail to the Party" in white letters on a red panel and hung it between two trees in the woods during the winter. We thought that if anybody was skiing by, he would do a double take, so we added the words "Strange that everything here

looks familiar, but I've never been in these parts." The idea that it should be written with white letters on a red field was mine. At first, I took part in the performances; then, because I had an infant, I hardly ever participated. I was hurt when I found out that in the first publications about the performances my name was not mentioned. This went on for a while, but then Andrei added it.

RB: In effect, you were invisible. Was this the same growing up in your family?

VK: I am in the third generation of a famous line of artists, and I feel the weight of family responsibility. I'm afraid to make mistakes. I have an obligation not to ruin my father's name. He was born to be an artist. My grandmother said that she was not about to waste her time giving birth to a bookkeeper. So he had to be an artist. My father was also expected to have a son to carry on the family name, but I was born. This is a traditional country when it comes to births. So my father had quite a jolt when I was born, but he expected the same type of accomplishment as if I had been a boy. He expected me to be a serious artist and not to use art as a diversion or as entertainment. My father considered everything that got in the way of art—me, the family—as an interruption.

RB: Personal life was secondary.

VK: He was brought up that way. It's easier for a man to realize this ambition than for a woman. If I had to make a choice between art and a child, I might not have chosen art. There really are not a lot of women artists in Russia. It's about our condition in life. Men are always the head of something. I do have a child, though. Monastirski is the father. We lived together for a long time, and our situation is classic. He's a poet and earned very little money. When our daughter was born, he worked in some administrative job in a museum. He barely earned enough for one person to live on. So I had to earn money for the three of us. I had studied at the Polygraphic Institute (where my grandfather and father had studied), so I worked in publishing, in layout and design. In Russia, parents often help out. My father, who didn't want me to get pregnant, helped us until the baby was born. In effect he said that if I wanted a baby, it was my decision and it would be my responsibility to manage as best I could. I was totally on my own.

RB: That was cruel.

VK: I would say so, but perhaps it was a service to me to be put in the position of sink or swim. Later, he had a change of heart and began to help me out because he realized that I was serious about art. I want to say that I don't judge him. I don't complain about him. He's my father and he has a right to his opinions whether I like his actions or not. That's how it is. But let me say that Andrei never saw himself in the role of a father. He was a poet and the baby was never a part of his way of living, his plan. I, on the other hand, had a strong desire to have a baby, preferably a girl. I think that men should give birth to boys. Having the baby gave me greater joy than making art. It was like a birthday party every day.

RB: You know, you are one of the very few artists who have said that having a baby was a great joy. Most complain about the difficulty of home life.

VK: Some say that men occupy themselves with cosmic questions. Maybe so. Women have to separate themselves into compartments—family, work. Men have different priorities. If a man is confronted with choices concerning fatherhood or work, he will chose work. It's a traditional choice.

RB: Let's go back to your schooling.

VK: There was no open discrimination, but the entrance examinations were something else. The authorities favored boys and tried to give them better grades. Part of the reason was that there were so many girls who wanted to attend. It's not healthy when there are too many girls. They squabble too much. Their competition is not about art, but about female things—romances, things like that. Teachers also favor the boys because the girls will drop out to have babies and not pursue their art careers. But I was psychologically geared to be an artist.

RB: What about your current work?

VK: I've become interested in a kind of sentimentality, a documentary sentimentalism. I'm interested in people's fate, their lives. I collect materials that have been left after they've gone. A few years ago, I received the Miturich family archives. It was huge. I then began to make collages from scraps of paper and photographs

RB: Do you have a circle of friends?

VK: Not an organized group. Anything like that becomes a threat to anybody who has lived through the Soviet period. The idea of an organization frightens me no end. I am an individualist in all regards. I want to do whatever I want to do. My friends are supportive, but we keep things informal.

Khlebnikova was not the only artist who told us that she was neither treated well nor properly acknowledged by her husband or partner. Irina Nakhova had a similar kind of experience that indicates the true indifference, even contempt, with which many Russian men view women. But before proceeding with Nakhova's interview, we want to include here the interview with Tatiana Faidish, who, like others, had experiences with her father and husband similar to those of Khlebnikova.

Tatiana Faidish

Tatiana Faidish (b. 1955) lives in Moscow and studied at the Surikov Art Institute. She began to paint in a nonrepresentational manner in 1990 and exhibits in shows organized by those concerned with women's issues. Although we have not included overly personal issues mentioned by the artists, we do want to say that Faidish, whose life is filled with tragedy, exemplifies the kind of willpower and determination that we found in most women we interviewed. At the end of her interview, Faidish said that she was in search of "the truth." We do not know precisely what this meant to her, but she revealed to us that her daughter, when sixteen years old, died under tragic circumstances, her current husband was dying from leukemia, and her three-year-old triplets had some serious medical and developmental issues. She is entirely self-supporting. This interview was given in 1995.

TF: Since my father died when I was twelve years old, I was raised by my mother. She was a very talented artist, but since my father was patriarchal, his relationship to women was condescending. He did not take them seriously. He believed that a woman's place was in the kitchen. When my father was alive, my mother did not paint at all. Inwardly, she wanted to realize herself as a person and as an artist. So she projected all her thwarted desires onto me. She believed that art came before anything else. I also have an older sister who is an artist. My father longed to have sons, and when I was born, things were bad in the family. My mother suffered because she had not given birth to a son, and my father became very depressed. During her pregnancy with me, she dreamed of having a boy. I was raised more like a boy than a girl. My father was very strict with me and knocked me around quite a lot. But I identified with him. He was a famous sculptor, Faidish-Krandievsky, and so I wanted to study art also.

RB: Do you like being a woman?

TF: A woman's life is a thousand times more complicated than a man's. I used to think that my personality was masculine. I suffered from it in that I wanted to be a man. I agonized over it during my childhood. I always played imaginary games and was always a male. Many women have such feelings. [A few others said as much in their interviews.] Of course, I got over them, and I came to understand that women possess an incredible richness of spirit and that it is great to be a woman.

RB: Is your husband an artist?

TF: My first husband was. We married when I was eighteen. For a time, we worked together as coauthors. But we divorced because of competition between us. When I started working independently, conflicts began. I continued in the style we had worked out together—which I believe that I developed. I came up with the ideas; he selected the colors. I became more successful and began to attract attention. In 1991, the State Tretiakov Gallery bought two of my paintings. This is a great honor for a Russian artist. Some other museums also bought my work, and I was invited to participate in international shows. My success upset him. But male artists do not treat women artists very well, anyway.

RB: Do you find differences between male and female artists?

TF: When a woman has an idea for a painting, she carries it out. Women work hard—in the home and at their art. But I think that for men the idea is enough to create and then they often agonize about it. Women are more steady. I think men should help out with the household. Perhaps their preoccupation with universal ideas gives them their freedom from family concerns, but this is really infantile behavior. If I had the time, I could also get involved in lots of ideas. Even so, I think that right now women artists are doing better work than the men.

RB: Are there any support groups for you?

TF: Yes, women artist friends. They are all very fine artists and help me spiritually and physically. We aren't political, but some of us have been in women's exhibitions both here and abroad.

Irina Nakhova

Irina Nakhova (b. 1955) has had a major career as an installation artist and as a painter and printmaker. At a very young age, during the 1970s and 1980s, she grew close to the dissident artists in Moscow. She now lives in the United States, and we have seen her several times. She has never told us about the following incident, but we will guess that it could still happen today.[5] In 1984, she presented four installations, called *Rooms,* in her apartment. Each room was covered with cutouts. Joseph Bakshstein, now the director of the Institute of Contemporary Art in Moscow, recorded visitors' responses. These were published, but he included only twelve responses, all by men. Whatever Nakhova's intent might have been, it was deflected, because the published responses were controlled by and through the masculine voice. In this interview, given in 1998, she takes some positions both similar to and opposite Khlebnikova's.

RB: Were you treated differently as a girl?

IN: I don't think so. We were all the children and grandchildren of Lenin and part of the machinery of the state. It was like—don't think, the state will take care of you. You have your duties and responsibilities, et cetera. There was also the ideology of equality. I felt suppressed as a person, but not because of gender. Everybody was suppressed.

RB: How about school?

IN: I didn't do things the traditional way. Through my parents, I met Victor Pivovarov [a dissident artist] when I was about thirteen and many of his friends [including Ilya Kabakov, Vladimir Yankilevsky, Edouard Shteinberg]. Years later, I wanted to go to the Polygraphic Institute because it was the most liberal school in Moscow. You only had to show up a few times a year to take exams. I spent about six years there working basically by myself. As for discrimination there and afterward, I was unaware and don't recall any. But I will say that I was very engrossed in my work and may have missed things. There were some women around and they were exceptional and persistent. On the street, there were always the catcalls—"Hey, pussy!" Whatever.

RB: What about shows?

IN: There were none in those days. I had something to do with the Collective Actions group which started in 1976. I took part in some of its events. But was never a collaborator. I didn't bring any ideas to them. I had married Andrei Monastirski in 1972 when I was eighteen years old. He led the group. We divorced about four years later. Neither one of us was family oriented and we each went our own way. We had a unique situation because everything was equal. "You want to eat food? Go and get it. We don't have any food? Go buy some." We were just too young to have gotten married. I also divorced my second husband, Joseph Bakshtein. He was very patriarchal, very male chauvinist. I had told him that I would never be a wifely kind of wife, that my work came first. He agreed, but of course he couldn't change. The end came when he decided to teach me how to paint. You know, we didn't split over gender issues. I just wanted to be myself, to find my own personality. Since we were all supposed to be equal, it probably never occurred to him or to other Russian men to think otherwise, to think in terms of women's needs or wants. It was not disrespect for the other gender, just disrespect for another person.

RB: Not because you are a woman?

IN: No. I don't think so.

RB: What about women in other fields?

IN: They were not in the top positions. Probably they were not allowed. I tried to stay out of all such situations. I never worked. I avoided all kinds of social situations both consciously and unconsciously. That's probably why I could survive as a person. I learned about these things when I came to America, but I was also aware in Russia about discrimination in general. Who cooked at home? My mother, not my father. This is everyday life. This did not affect me in my adult life, because I never cooked. I often asked my mother why she did not divorce my father. They are still together fifty or sixty years later. It's some kind of co-dependence. I don't accept that. By the way, she makes more money than he does in her job.

RB: What do you think of the women who gave up their professions for their husbands?

IN: I don't know. I cannot possibly imagine this situation, because I'm alone and I'm alone consciously, and I chose this way, because in Russia it was not possible to find a partner who could understand you properly. And here [in the United States] it is the same. You need your space. I want to be on my own, I want to live my own life. It's very rare that people live their own lives. They always live somebody's life—their children's their husband's, their grandparents', their lover's.

RB: Do you think you can be married and still live your own life?

IN: It's pure luck if you can. People I know wanted children. I never had children and never wanted to have any because I knew what it was about. Either that or you would have to be very wealthy and have nannies rather than a husband to help raise the children. Today, we are still living by our body instincts—our belly instincts, our genital instincts—but not our brain instincts. We have to educate people so that neither the penis nor the vagina rules the world. The feminist movement is a first step.

RB: Tell me about these sculptures. One looks like a David figure and the other one is in female dress?

IN: She's Aphrodite. In this installation, there are five male and five female images wearing differently sized coats and I've mixed up the male and female coats. I wanted to say that it does not matter, that it is the personality that counts. Sometimes a male will talk in a female voice and vice versa. I want to bring to the museum level what our society is about—homophobia, racism, antisemitism, antifeminism. I don't want to transcend the body, but I do want to have a brain that views the body on the human level. But we still live on the basic instinct level. If we could think with our brains then we could say that it is wonderful to have a penis or a vagina, that it is respected, and that each of us is respected as a whole being. But I don't think it will happen.

RB: Is there any hope for Russia?

IN: Who knows what happens there? In Russia, for example, I might not be hired by a university because I am from the intelligentsia. A person from the working class would stand a better chance of a job. This is a class thing. But if there will be layoffs, women will go first.

Nakhova's work, as she described here, sometimes deals with gender issues or cultural constructions of individual personalities. We were not able to determine if this was part of the American phase of her career or if this kind of imagery was developed in Russia. As this interview suggests, it does not take women long to tap into their anger and into their past or present confusion about notions of equality, especially when they are confronted in one-on-one conversations about gender issues. There are many such stories we could report here, but two more will suffice, one by Gulbakhar Ashimova, from Uzbekistan, whose encounters with men in Central Asia were probably worse than those experienced by Russian women; and the other by Irina Mozhaeva, who found that in Moscow, women could be just as exploitative and oppressive.

Gulbakhar Ashimova

Gullbakhar Ashimova (b. 1951) was born in eastern Turkestan, lived in Kazakhstan, and then moved to Uzbekistan. She paints fanciful figures in a very colorful style, invoking feelings of life, vitality, and a joyous sense of creative renewal (fig. 31). This interview was given in New York in 1996.

GA: I was born in eastern Turkestan. My father was a master of musical instruments and was called the Stradivarius of the East. The musical atmosphere in my father's house was important to me and to my sisters, who are dancers and actresses, and to my brother, who also makes musical instruments.

RB: When and where did you begin your art education?

GA: We moved to Kazakhstan in 1963, where I received my education, and then my family moved to Tashkent in 1971, where I studied dramatic arts. Basically, I am self-taught because my teachers in Kazakhstan did not think my work was academic enough. My teachers were all

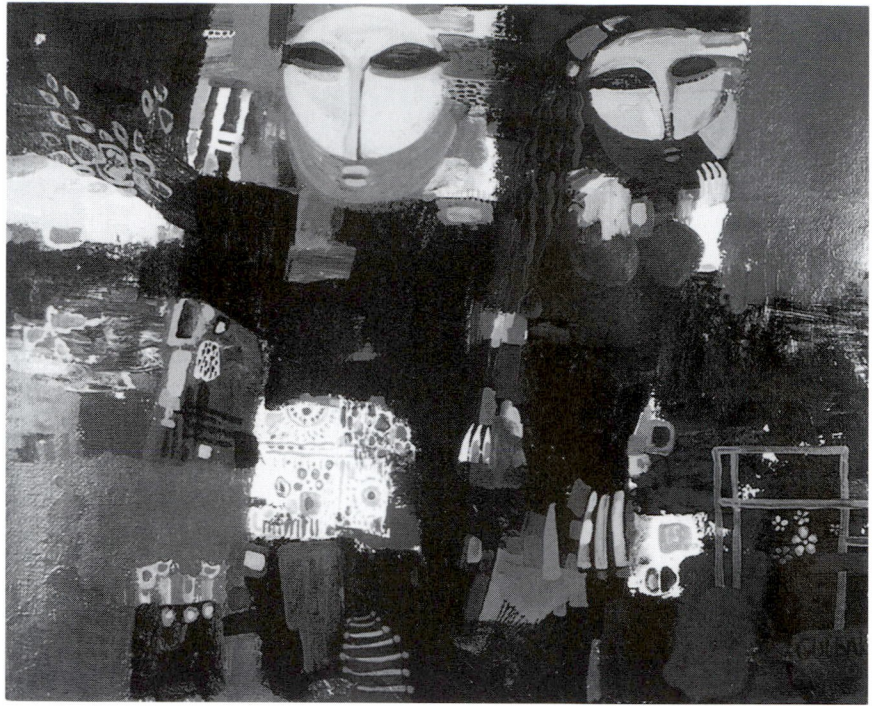

31. Gulbakhar Ashimova, *Day and Night,* 1994, acrylic on canvas. (Courtesy Gulbakhar Ashimova.)

men who liked to drink a lot. My graphics teachers were Russians and Jews. They had a different attitude from my painting teachers, who were Uzbekis. We have many women poets in Central Asia but only about two women artists. The attitude there is that there is something dirty about being a woman artist. It is something a woman should not do. I experienced discomfort, but I lived my own life as I chose. I could not socialize with the male artists nor could I feel comfortable with them. They were also very condescending and would say things like, "Gulia is a nice woman. All she has to do is smile and all will go well."

RB: And your family?

GA: They were supportive. But outside the family, I always felt that I was treated differently from the men. I was a member of the union, but I couldn't ask for help. Men, of course, used all the privileges the union gave to them. It's very difficult when a woman tries to express her individuality in Middle Asia. It's better in Russia; the Muslim world is different.

RB: How did you earn a living?

GA: I worked at home as an illustrator for publishers.

RB: Do you have any children?

GA: I have a daughter. Her father is a very famous Muslim painter, a painter laureate of the state who was very self-centered and never helped me. There was no man who really understood me. And, besides, our artists are alcoholics. Here in America, I feel I can overcome any condition.

RB: What about your art?

GA: I just began to paint nudes. I believe that women are the bearers of spiritual beauty and of the future. In women, I see everything. They are the beginning of creation and of all understanding. I want to suggest the idea that women are the guardians of the world, of the home, and of nature. They hold the world in their hands and they are connected to the sun and the moon. I want to elevate the image of women to the highest realm. I rarely include men in my pictures.

It is interesting to note that whatever else they do and do not have in common, Ashimova and Khlebnikova have idolized their own sense of womanhood. Both love and thoroughly enjoy the process of motherhood, and they think of women as central to the health and continuation of the universe. Rather than rage against men and their experiences with men, each has withdrawn in her own way within the parameters of an idealized feminine world and has established a comfort zone there. In similar fashion, Anita Meldere (b. 1949), one of Latvia's most successful artists, said, in a published interview on the occasion of a retrospective of her work, that she wanted to express the workings of her soul.

> Women—loving, loved, unloved, woman of fortitude, woman of frailty, woman—Tossed by conflicting emotions. Woman's feelings, the mothering instinct. It is one's own life experience that underlies and permeates one's creative career, this particularly applies to a woman artist.[6]

First, no man would allow his work or his motivation to be described in Meldere's language. It would only reinforce his belief in the superiority—that is, the intellectual basis—of his own art and the emotionality of women's art. Second, a complicated and unresolvable situation arises when it is realized that by lionizing the experiences of motherhood and by idealizing women's spiritual qualities, these artists unconsciously perpetuate, in effect, the old Soviet belief systems about motherhood and domesticity—if not about being productive workers for the state. The language of Khlebnikova and Ashimova was such that it was clear that they had children for their own pleasure and not for patriotic reasons, and that they raised their children for the sheer delight in doing so. Given the context of the Soviet society in which they were brought up, they reclaimed their rights of reproduction for themselves, yet their idealization of their role as mothers nevertheless kept alive the Soviet ideology of motherhood. This is quite opposite the positions taken by Zvezdocheteva, Nakhova, and Mitrofanova.

Irina Mozhaeva

Irina Mozhaeva (b. 1960) was the only artist who admitted to belonging to any kind of group of women artists. (At least one other interviewee belonged to a group, but neglected to mention it during our interview. We came upon her name and an illustration of her painting in a catalogue of that group. Clearly, she wanted to suppress that information.) Mozhaeva belonged to Irida, a group formed in 1991 that sold paintings by women. We are presenting here Mozhaeva's side of the story, which is horrendous. During an exhibition and sale that took place in the United States, the publicity was entirely positive.[7] This interview was given in 1998.

> **IM:** I was born in Siberia on the Enisei River. My father was from the Tulsk region. My parents moved to Moscow when I was ten years old. I went to the Academy of Textiles and graduated in 1984. It was good there because we could work in abstract styles and say that we were making decorative art designs. We were obliged to work in our chosen specialty for three years. I worked in a factory in which I could design and make scarves. I learned to paint on silk. Our teachers were mostly men, but the dean of faculties was a woman and women played an important role in the humanities program. After I graduated, I didn't join the union. Most of the weaker students did in order to get commissions, a studio, and exhibitions. I was able to manage on my own. With perestroika, alternative unions were started. First I joined something called Arm-Mirazh, a union of professional artists. Then I joined the Union of Woman Artists, the official name for Irida. I was a member for a number of years. We felt it was like part of a women's rebellion to belong. In the regular unions, men were always dominant and abused their positions. A young woman artist had to resort to all kinds of means to join, like sleeping with some official. I would never lower myself in any way to

become a union member. When I joined Irida, we were about ten or fifteen women. We talked about how nobody would be able to oppress us any longer, how we would organize ourselves, how we would organize both Russian and international exhibitions. Unfortunately, about four or five women seized control, and the rest of us were once again without any power, just rank-and-file members of a group of artists. For example, when we were organizing a show that would travel to Paris, there was an argument about who would take the pictures. The leaders said that they would. Then they began to dictate what I should make for the exhibition, which works would be acceptable and which would not, which would sell, which would be liked. Our selling price was to be no more than fifty dollars. Artists were not allowed to set their own prices. Then we were told to make matrioshka dolls [the dolls within dolls]. The leaders behaved like men. Four of them went to Paris for a month with the show. I showed my irritation, so they told me to sell my work on my own. We had endless meetings like in Soviet times. We had to get together every two weeks. I missed two meetings and I was threatened with expulsion. Then I left Irida. But I know that the leadership began to live very well. They even stopped painting because they had become so rich. They began to live the good life. The rest of us were like laborers. Later, they organized salons. At first, everything seemed fine, but then the same things more or less happened. All of this is very upsetting. It was an absolute injustice to have to sell through them at the prices they had set. I mean, they gave us a price, but we never knew what they sold a work for. People could not get money from them for works that were sold. They said that they had already spent the money, that they didn't have it yet, come back in six months. Those who could leave, left. I have enough commissions on which to live without them. I have had no desire to look into any other women's organizations since then.

RB: Early in Irida's history, what did you discuss before things became impossible?

IM: We discussed how men discriminated against us, how they have made us second-class citizens. Recently, I went to an exhibit of male artists. One asked me where I had studied, and he said, "Oh, I see. You're making women's art." In fact, many men went to the Academy of Textiles. I want to tell you that I began to meet with a small group of women here in my studio. It began when I told some women that I would teach them how to paint. Suddenly, it clicked, and I became the informal leader of an informal group. Many had problems at home and needed a place to air their grievances. They really needed a support group. But we recently disbanded because we could not afford to keep it going.

RB: What did they complain about?

IM: Their husbands objected when they left the house for a few hours. They wanted them home where they belonged. Many women felt an inner loneliness, a spiritual aloneness, a lack of communication with everybody. Within the family, they felt that nobody understood one another. Their husbands thought of them as workhorses. We would sometimes help one another with our children. We're all about forty years old and we're having our various crises. It is a tough time personally and economically. But on the whole, we all try to keep our sense of humor. We love life and want to be creative. We try not to mope around. I often go to Germany, where I am amazed at the luxurious lives women lead there but who seem so sad spiritually.

RB: Are you married?

IM: For thirteen years, but for the past five, we've been having problems—all connected with my work. We have contact with each other, but we no longer have a marriage. He says that when I went back to work five years ago, it took over all other considerations, that I abandoned the family. In some ways, I agree, even though he initially encouraged me to get back to work. When I had my child, I was totally immersed in motherhood, and he thought I should continue with my painting. He promised to take care of our daughter, and now he has forgotten all that. I guess my work now takes too much of my time.

RB: Did he object to your success?

IM: I noticed that after perestroika, women proved to be more flexible then our men. We adapted quicker to the new situation. Everything was in a chaotic state. Men took all this very hard, while the women rolled with it. A woman I know who was an engineer works now as a housekeeper. She has to support her family. He husband could not change and adjust. When my husband became unemployed, our troubles really began. I sold very well and he couldn't deal with that. I had no choice but to keep working. He said that we had enough money to live on if we were careful. But how much is enough? Perhaps I should have paid more attention to his emotional needs, but I had to work. He was a scientist who did research on rockets.

Mozhaeva experienced firsthand, and outlined for us, the fears that many have concerning women's organizations—meetings, bureaucracy, instructions, loss of freedom, no or minimal immediate financial gains. In effect—"What's the point?" She also revealed the incredible need Russian women have for some kind of networking at least on an informal neighborhood level, and also the resignation they all acknowledge in face of overwhelmingly difficult conditions at home and in the workplace.

Ludmila Gorlova

Ludmila Gorlova (b. 1968) had just turned thirty when we interviewed her in 1998, but she had already been recognized as a significant young artist-photographer by virtue of her exhibitions at the XL [Ex El] Gallery in Moscow. She was also included in the important exhibitions in St. Petersburg and Moscow 1999 titled *Gender Boundaries* and *Anamnesis Lapsus Memoriae (Remembrances Are the Mistakes of Memory)* mentioned earlier, in the Brief Chronology. She studied at the In Memory of 1905 Art School in Moscow.

LG: What I do tends toward a feminist position, but I do not consider myself a feminist. We don't have a special women's organization yet, and I do socialize with other artists, both men and women. We all suffer shock and stress from the speed with which things are changing. We can't catch our breath or even understand what's going on. I can say that I think things will get worse for women because of the economic situation, because of employment opportunities. For jobs, women have to be between certain ages now, have no children, dress in a sexy way, like in a short skirt. For us this is a nightmare. For our mothers, it is terrible. But I have not come up against any discrimination because we were raised in a society of equality. Discrimination was unthinkable. When I first started to exhibit in 1987 in artist union shows, I was never put down by men. Even if something like that did happen, I had enough strength of character to defend myself. The law was on my side.

RB: How do you see your own work today?

LG: If people see my work as that of a woman, then so be it. We consider feminine works to be signs of weakness here.

RB: What about your work called *And Quiet Flows the Don*?

LG: It is a novel in photos after the novel by Mikhail Sholokhov, the Soviet writer. The novel has suddenly become popular. There is now a real desire to remember the past after the onslaught of new ideologies, advertisements, and our new way of life. We need to get in touch with ourselves, so there is a desire to look at old Soviet films and books in order to reconstruct our memories. We need to compare who we were then and who we are now. The hero of the novel is a Cossack farmer who finds himself in a situation between the reds and the whites [the revolutionaries and the counterrevolutionaries]. He wanders back and forth between the two sides and feels comfortable with neither. He can't find his way. This is what is happening now. What do we keep of the old, what do we accept of the new? So we need to understand the past more objectively than in the early 1990s. Then, we were angry with the changes. We thought we would have paradise. Now it is clear that this won't happen. So we are beginning to see some positive aspects of the Soviet past. Not everything was horrible before perestroika. So in my photographs, I posed people as if they were living as Cossacks and were engaged in various activities. It's like a historical re-creation of a past time—some clichés based on the old ways of life as well as on our own. I think there is also in it a sense of the inability to adapt to new situations.

RB: Where did the idea for this work come from?

LG: Last year, I was in the depths of the provinces and began to take pictures with no plan in mind. Then I realized that things were like a comic strip. At a gathering, a government functionary appeared and sang a monarchist hymn, people sang a Soviet hymn, a partisan song, and Yiddish songs. Everything happened at once. I became inspired by the absurdity of it all. I wanted to express the drama behind that situation. So my Cossacks are like a joke, a link with the past in comic-book style.

There are no particular feminist elements in Gorlova's version of *And Quiet Flows the Don*. In it she explores and improvises on its cultural and political implications. In her interview, she also distanced herself from feminism. But in an instance in which she, as others, do not always realize the implications of their own work, she collaborated with Anna Alchuk (see interview) in 1997, a year before the *Don* photographs were made, on a series of send-ups of photo stills from Soviet movies, titled *The Exaltation Spaces*. These images were included in the exhibitions in 1999 in St. Petersburg and Moscow mentioned previously. In them, she and Alchuk imitated the poses taken by the actors. This is what they had to say about their photographs:

It proved interesting for us to investigate [the] homoeroticism that is latently present in most of the Stalin-era films. From the 1930s to the 1950s, it was prohibited to openly show, to put on the screen, signs of heterosexual sensuality. As a result, we have a substantial number of homosexual kisses and embraces that serve as a replacement of repressed sensuality. An attempt to tackle those Stalin-epoch film stills in a new, contemporary vein consists not in the replacement of actor's faces and bodies by ours, but in introducing a would-be psychodrama between two women characters.[8]

By the time of the exhibition she must have realized that these photographs not only challenged traditional gender-derived roles during Stalin's era, but such roles in contemporary society as well. For example, in one still, taken from the movie *Far from the Motherland,* a woman dressed in a military uniform has just killed another woman, who is also dressed in a uniform. No doubt, one figure is meant to be Russian and the other, German. Both are clearly involved in "men's" work.

Gorlova also completed a project in 1994 titled *Happy Childhood.* It is in its way a much mellower critique of birthing conditions than those done just a few years earlier by Elena Elagina and the Peppers (see Brief Chronology and fig. 2). Gorlova, understanding and accepting the fact that it was impossible either to change traditional notions of male power and female submission or to improve hospital conditions, thought that an appropriate task for art was to be ameliorative and helpful rather than provocative and revolutionary. So, as a gesture to ease the trauma of childbirth for both mother and child (conditions are said to be still horrible for mothers and babies), Gorlova exhibited works in a maternity ward, her efforts including presenting video tapes and sending postcards to the mothers. She wanted to help them overcome depression, phobia of their infants, humiliation, and absolute dependence on the hospital staff. In the catalogue for the exhibition, Alexandra Obukhova wrote that Gorlova knew that her piece could change neither the minds nor the situations of the mothers and babies, and that her gesture was utopian, but that she wanted to create it, anyway.[9] One wonders whether Gorlova would be so gentle if she returned to this theme today. In any event, we can observe in her work the kind of radical change that, according to Kamenetskaia, has taken place at the end of the decade.

We have arbitrarily placed the remaining interviews at the end of this chapter. Two are with artist couples and two with gallery owners. We use the term "artist couples" to mean two different things—couples who work together as a team and husbands who insisted on being present at the interviews. We include interviews with Elena Elagina and Igor Makarevich, probably the most important artist couple in Russia today, and the second with Tatiana Arzamasova and Lev Evzovich. We then report on three interviews in which the husbands insisted on being present and who interfered (one totally) with the interviews. (A fourth husband, the important dissident artist Francesco Infante, who was in the room when we began, graciously left at the request of his wife, Nonna Goriunova.) We include this material after the interviews with Elagina and Arzamasova not because it is either sad or amusing, depending on one's point of view, but because it speaks to the issues women artists face. As smart as they may be, as well educated as they may be, as good artistically as they might be, they are constantly reminded of their place in the family hierarchy. The men were beyond embarrassment and seemed to have absolutely no self-awareness of what they were doing other than that they were both asserting and defending their role in the family unit.

Elena Elagina

Elena Elagina (b. 1949) works both independently and collaboratively with her husband, Igor Makarevich. Although they both make two-dimensional pieces, they are best known for their sculptures and installations. Both have been in involved with the Collective Actions group since the late 1970s, and both have exhibited in western Europe and the United States. In her interview, Elagina alludes directly to a serious problem in trying to work out a chronology of women's art shows and of feminist developments in the art world. There is hardly a paper trail in the way of brochures or catalogues or magazine articles. Memories are poor, and dates are vague. This interview was given in 1997.

EE: We have participated in many efforts by Collective Actions since 1979. Igor and I organized a two-person performance on one occasion and wrote scripts for others. I was the only woman in the group at that time, and we considered ourselves to be totally equal. Later, other women participated.

RB: Do you always work with Igor?

EE: Lately. Really only since the beginning of the 1990s.

IM: Lena was educated as a philologist, so she is extremely sensitive to semantics. Art containing words comes easy to her. I have more talent for the plastic arts. I can give form to ideas that occur from the reading of a text. In this sense, we are an ideal pair. We complement each other. But we do have rules.

EE: Problems do arise, since nothing is problem free.

RB: Many women artists have told us that women approach art on a more emotional level than men, that men are more rational. Do you think so?

EE: Speaking for myself, I believe it is the other way around, that men are more emotional. It is lodged in the way we view the world. Women can deal with big issues. This is not always possible at least for me because I never have enough time—household chores. This is why Igor

and I work so well together. I'll come up with an idea and he'll finish it.
RB: You are saying that how one thinks is a question of how much time you can devote to the idea in question.
EE: Yes. Time makes a big difference.
IM: I lean toward a romantic worldview, one filled with pathos. I like romantic literature and am concerned with aesthetic issues. I lean toward Baudelaire and Verlaine. Lena is more ironic and thinks differently from me.
EE: I don't like romanticism at all. But because of that and other things, we are harmonious and balance each other.
RB: Elena, how about your schooling?
EE: I don't remember any differences in educational approach to boys and girls. Girls tended to be better students. Some teachers preferred girls because they were better behaved. I went to the Moscow Art School from 1962 to 1967, but I spent a lot of time during those years working with Ernst Neizvestny [a major dissident sculptor] when he still lived in Moscow. That's where I got my education. I was not a member of the union, so I hardly exhibited before perestroika—some apartment shows, that's all. I think working with Neizvestny got me in more trouble than anything else. I was turned down by an art school because of my association with him.
RB: Are there women's groups in Moscow?
EE: We have too many other worries to be involved in that. But we did try to do a few women's shows around 1990. I remember a male curator put on a show, but he ripped us off. Another show I was in was called *The Woman Worker* [mentioned in the Alchuk interview]. It was the very first women's show in our circle of artists. That was sometime in the early 1990s. Joseph Bakshtein curated a show and played a dirty trick on us. He and Konstantin Zvezdochetov [Zvezdochetova's former husband] showed their work using women's pseudonyms. Then we had a show called *Four Hearts* in 1992. Again, Bakshtein curated it. Although the women in it did what they wanted, the show was dedicated to a man. There was a show called *The Visit*. Each woman found a character. I chose a scientist from Stalin's time. Her name was Olga Lepeshinskaia. She was something of a feminist in her time because when she decided to become a biologist, women were not allowed to enter the university. She was probably the only woman scientist at that time. She was not a very good scientist. We should really call her an alchemist. She said she discovered a way to rejuvenate people so that they could live to be two hundred years old. Stalin loved her.
RB: What about today?

EE: It's difficult for women to get together, but now we have several women gallery curators—Lena Romanova, Lena Serina, Nina Zaretskaia [see interviews with last two]—but no real commercial galleries. As for a feminist movement, it is still rather artificial because we are not entirely clear about the issues.

RB: Let me ask you if you think there is a difference in the way men and women make art.

EE: Perhaps, but because of our ideological training, we were taught there are no differences. But of course it was always harder for women because of our double burden—at work and in the home. Maybe in my work differences do appear through choice of materials or objects, things that are connected with women. Perhaps there is something unconscious.

IM: In our country, women's art is not channeled by sexual differences.

EE: I don't see anything specifically female in art today. But I would say that women have a strong connection to nature and men can be more pragmatic as well as emotional. But I see what you're driving at, and I cannot distinguish between women's art and feminist art.

Tatiana Arzamasova

Tatiana Arzamasova (b. 1955) works and exhibits with her husband and another man as a trio. They are figurative painters and have exhibited in western Europe. Some work is composed of academically styled, erotic nudes. The work reproduced here is from a series in which each partner is seen slitting his or her own throat (fig. 32). This interview dates from 1995.

TA: I don't think that a difference between male and female artists exists. In their interactions with society, gender is not an issue. Perhaps women's perceptions are more sensitive, even more superficial, but interactions with society are identical.

RB: Do you think there is any difference in their art?

TA: No, but of course there is some difference. I don't mean an obvious feminist orientation as in the West, but during Soviet times, there were theories about motherhood, and with that went portraits of loved ones. I don't experience any feminine bias. Perhaps this is lost in the dialogue I have with my husband, Lev.

RB: Was the ideology of equality real or just rhetoric?

TA: It was official, but it had no effect on me. We were trained as architects.

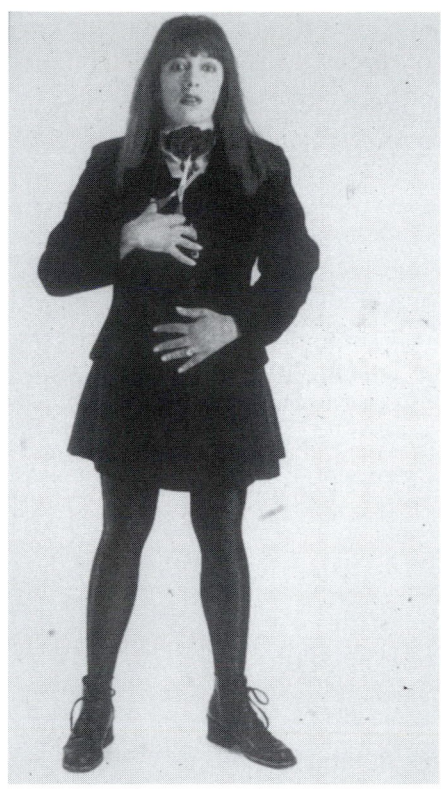

32. Tatiana Arzamasova, *Violence,* 1995, oil on canvas. (Courtesy Tatiana Arzamasova.)

RB: I mean in regard to your spiritual and psychological development.
TA: In Moscow, everything is male concentrated. There is no discussion right now regarding women artists. We don't have any women stars as in America. Recently, there was an interest in body art here, but I don't know of any woman who works with that anymore. Most contemporary shows are only of male artists. There is not one woman avant-gardist now. It's a very masculine scene now. It goes without saying that I want recognition, but it requires very aggressive behavior.
RB: How do you work together?
TA: We are a group of three—myself, Lev, and Evgenii Sviatskii. I work with two men and seldom feel that my voice is not heard. Lev usually initiates the dialogue between us.
RB: Do you have the same amount of time for your work as Lev does?
TA: Our son was born in 1982. I try to run the household. It is traditional here. I do the dishes. If we should become rich and famous, our first purchase will be a dishwasher.

RB: When I ask such questions, women ask if I am a feminist and their tone suggests that it is something terrible.

TA: I support what you say, but the reality of our situation here is different. It stays the same. Small steps are being taken here. You can see it in the new tolerance for sexual minorities.

RB: And in your work?

YA: We work as a team, which is the way architects work. Our third person, Evgenii, acts as a buffer to whom we can turn. We feel tensions, but this is at the basis of joint work. I cannot imagine living with a man with whom I could not have a creative dialogue.

RB: Has your husband been invited to show his work, but not yours?

TA: Practically never since we began to work together in 1989. But of course there are moments of envy and jealousy. One time, Lev had an opportunity to make a design for an interesting site in Tel Aviv. Speaking honestly, I was very upset and disappointed for both personal and artistic reasons that he tried to do it by himself. The matter resolved itself when the work was stopped.

RB: Have you ever felt discrimination?

TA: I remember one incident when we were working on a design and were introduced to the people in charge. In English it would translate as "here is the stud and here is his bitch" or "here is the tomcat and his she cat." I wasn't insulted, because I know my country. I know this is disgusting, but the tradition here is that men relate to women in a negative way. It's normal, the same old boorish set of attitudes.

RB: Do you create works from a sense of your own femininity?

TA: Times are changing and we have to develop a new language, but there is nothing feminine in my work. But in our new era, it is permissible for a woman to become a man psychologically. But I have no desire to give up my female essence.

RB: What about this work [see fig. 32]?

TA: We dedicated this work to traditional male-female relationships. There is always tension between and a limited openness between the sexes. When one gets to the last degree of openness and candid interchange, then one approaches the borderline of self-destruction and violence. So this work is ironic in that we each are cutting our own throats. But there are literally threads placed between each of the figures [between each canvas] connecting them to each other. The same scissors that can cut threads and fingernails can also cut throats.

Arzamazova did not understand when we tried to explain that perhaps their images of self-mutilation were sublimated images of mutilation of the other. She seemed to be quite innocent of the kind of psychological insight we take for granted in the West. Her feeling was that this particular work was ironic, and that was all there was to it. Her various contradictory thoughts throughout the interview also indicated to us that she had not fully worked through the old double message of equality and equal rights. It goes without saying that she was not alone in this regard.

A further word about architecture as a career for women. In 1998, we interviewed two young architecture students at the Repin Art Academy in St. Petersburg, Dasha Zakhunova (b. 1977) and Ani Simonian (b. 1978). Both said that they lacked the necessary energy men possessed in order to become architects as well as the kind of mental strength needed to cope with the politics of a male-dominated field. Despite good and important family connections within the field, both thought that they might ultimately work as interior designers or landscape architects.

With regard to other couples who have either worked together or who critique each other's efforts, virtually all acknowledged and accepted the leading roles played by their husbands. Some said that they were the idea persons and their husbands worked out the details. Still others said that they had given up their art from time to time to attend to domestic chores. All complained about such chores.

A few husbands insisted on being present at the interviews. Some were helpful in clarifying points and remained more or less in the background (especially Elena Korennova's and Zoya Frolova's husbands), but some did not. The most threatened was the husband of Arte Dumpe (b. 1933), perhaps the leading sculptor of public monuments in Latvia. He is a professor of linguistics at Riga University. When we met, he immediately announced in English that feminism was trash and that he had no respect for anybody associated with it. Then he said that since his wife did not speak Russian, he would speak to us in English and translate into Latvian for her. He then crafted all of her statements into bland responses that probably reflected his opinions. At the end of the interview, Arte Dumpe turned to Renee and said quietly, so that her husband would not hear, that she spoke Russian perfectly and that he had forbidden her to use it during our meeting.

The interview with Nina Kotyel (b. 1950s), a Moscow-based artist, was also distressing. She has been included in all-women exhibitions and is known to those with feminist leanings. Her paintings often include large-scale images of food—fruits and vegetables that she paints in a semi–pop art style (see fig. 3). She says that she uses items she looks at, cooks, and eats every day. Her husband, Vladimir Salnikov, has been photographed in feminist projects by Anna Alchuk (see interview), but during Kotyel's interview he positioned himself on a high stool behind his wife as if he were the ventriloquist and she the dummy. This is not a fanciful image, since he constantly interfered, interrupting her answers and insisting on speaking for her. He could not be stopped, at least by our polite requests. But even if he had been silent, it became clear that she could not have answered any questions with honesty in his presence.

In an interview with the Estonian artist Marje Uksine in 1995, her husband simply took over the conversation and could not be stopped, even as he prated on about the number and importance of women in that country's art world. It is no exaggeration to say that at the end of the interview, Uksine's face and body language revealed that she had become very upset by the fact that her voice literally had been stilled and that neither she nor we had been able to do anything about it.

We met Valera (b. 1948) and Natalia (b. 1958) Cherkashin in New York in 1997. They work together as photographers, and so they gave a joint interview. One did not have to be a feminist lawyer to notice how, without realizing it, he continually incriminated himself. It was not just in the choice of words—when she referred to a point of collision between them, he used the word "watershed," nor in his insistence that gender issues have been eliminated from their work, nor even in his proclamation that she had not suffered because she is a woman, nor in his acknowledgment that women are stronger and do not struggle as men do. It was rather in his assertion that Russian women want to be women, 100 percent women, that *that* was their ideal. Feminists, he held, have failed to be 100 percent women. A feminist usually did not have a happy life, so somebody had to be blamed. "In Russia, " he said, "if a woman is a feminist, it is assumed that things did not work out for her in her life." A Russian woman, to be valued, had to take on a heavy load. This was tradition. We then tried but failed to explain to him that he was blaming the victim for the problems that men had imposed. We mention all this not to lambaste Cherkashin and the other husbands, but to make the point that theirs seem to be common modes of thought among the men with whom we spoke and as reported by many interviewees.

We interviewed a few gallery owners in addition to Aidan Salakhova (see interview). Since their interests were market driven, they had little to say about women's issues. But we have included some of their comments, which throw light on a few of the problems that artists faced in the 1990s.

Nina Zaretskaia

Nina Zaretskaia is the director of the Telegalery in Moscow, one of the few avant-garde galleries in that city. This interview was given in 1995.

NZ: I want to show you a video of Alena Martinova shaving her public hair [see interview]. It is filled with irony and plays up women's weaknesses and vulnerability, but it also makes a tough feminist statement about women's rights to do whatever they want with their bodies. It also expresses a negative view of all kinds of beauty products. This is still a new kind of thing in Moscow and it takes guts for a woman to express herself that way. I look at her as a kind of primitive trying to make contemporary art. She does not introspect nor does she build on theoretical models. She simply acts out her feelings and the necessity to express them in gestures.

RB: Are there other performance artists who use video?

NZ: There are some, mostly men.

RB: Are there any feminist organizations yet?

NZ: No, nor support groups. Women artists are not organized. Some women participate in group shows or exhibit with their husbands. But the men assume a superior position.

RB: Women seem to be opposed to any organizations, as though they are ashamed of such groups.

NZ: Well, in our society, men are dominant. It's hard for a woman artist like Martinova to show without her husband's consent. So she made him coauthor of some of her works. When a woman is alone here, she encounters barriers. If she's with her husband, nobody speaks to her. So I guess we need a woman's organization to take care of various formalities. Perhaps it might help with family problems, as well. I think people in St. Petersburg are more politically correct. There is interest there in feminism and homosexual art. But here in Moscow, conceptual art is dominant. On the other hand, I think there is more honesty among women artists today in revealing more about their private lives in their art.

Zaretsky's main point seemed to be that feminism might be good for the art business if it would lead to organizations that would, in effect, handle administrative matters and help alleviate home conditions. This sounded very practical to us as a way to circumvent theoretical issues that many seemed to reject.

Elena Selina

Selina and Serge Khripon are directors of the XL (Ex El) Gallery in Moscow, perhaps the major avant-garde gallery in that city. It occupies what appears to be a small shed in the back court of an office building. This interview was given in 1997. Since the directors agreed on all points discussed, we use only Selina's initials.

RB: Are there any women's art organizations in Moscow?

ES: Only Natalia Kamenetskaia's Idioma.

RB: Are there more female artists than male?

ES: Traditionally, men have dominated the scene. About that, there is nothing to say. In Moscow, there are a lot of women artists, but not too many are capable of working with abstract ideas. It is still hard to find ten who can develop such ideas. What we mean is that they do not produce highly theoretical or intellectual art. We are waiting for them to get up to the same level as the men. Instead, many go into decorative art, into superficial arts and crafts. There are only a few who produce actual works of art. We're not interested in art that represents women's issues.

RB: Why are young women interested in representing the male body?

ES: We had a problem with body art. For a long time, conceptualism was dominant—from 1993 to 1996—and then there was a wave of artists in rebellion, men especially, who ran around naked, howling. Now, artists don't have to go to such extremes to attract attention. Right now, we think the men are showing more energy than the women. Alena Romanova, Natalia Nesterova, and Irina Nakhova are among the only strong women artists. Others, like Ludmila Gorlova and Tania Liberman, are finding their way. They are all signature artists. [All are interviewed in this book.]

RB: Is there a woman's subject matter?

ES: They are interested in love and the body now. Women are more visual and less theoretical than men, and women are more interested in actuality, in real-life situations, than in working out feminist problems. They also want to be considered on the same professional level as men and being a feminist wouldn't help. For example, Idioma gets no financial support from women, because they don't like to think of themselves as oppressed.

Conclusions

IN THE preceding chapters we discussed aspects of the lives of about forty artists of the eighty-two who were interviewed. Since many artists gave similar answers to our questions, we have not mentioned or included excerpts from all the interviews. The questions we asked dealt broadly with training, family life, kinds of subject matter explored, attitudes toward men, and interests in women's issues. We also asked about life before and after the collapse of Communism. Our conclusions are tentative for obvious reasons—we did not explore a particular cohort in terms of art style, social ideology, or age group. We did not venture outside major cities. But nevertheless, we did hear certain notions, points of view, and experiences mentioned repeatedly so that we feel some reasonable conclusions can be drawn from the material we gathered.

Many reported that their mothers rather than their fathers encouraged them to become artists. Training generally started in special grade schools for gifted students and continued in art institutes when they had become young adults. These institutes could be either fine-arts or decorative-arts institutes. This was the usual path, but several became artists, sometimes because their boyfriends were artists or because they decided at some point in their lives to become artists. Fathers were often opposed because they thought their daughters would drop out and have babies or because they did not think women should be artists at all. They were also disappointed when their wives gave birth to girl children. Mothers who were artists themselves tended to be more helpful than fathers who were artists. Overall, several owed their success to having a strong mother.

Older artists insisted that they never experienced discrimination or unequal treatment in art schools even as they recalled memories of boys being pushed ahead of them and of a lack of women teachers in advanced courses, especially in fine-arts courses. They maintained that there was equality under the law, so discrimination was impossible. Some justified their beliefs by telling us that because of the war, fewer men than women studied art in the 1940s and 1950s. Those men who did study may not have been the strongest artists, either because they lacked sufficient talent or because they had been psychologically weakened as a result of their experiences in the war as well as from the general Soviet repression of individuality, which affected women to a lesser degree.

Younger women acknowledged some discrimination, but some still preferred to study with male teachers even though their teachers often discouraged them from continuing their studies. The general consensus was that many women students did drop out or, after graduation, gave up their careers for family responsibilities. When in school, they were also discouraged from studying in monumental-painting departments because it was physically too taxing. Evidently, as a result of equal rights, women were responsible for lugging around their own heavy, large picture frames and canvases, but because they were women, they were considered too weak to do so, one of several tautologies we encountered. Teachers also often treated women students in a condescending manner, accepting the notion that men were rational and intellectual, while women were emotional and not as able to think as deeply as men. Several women simultaneously accepted and rejected this notion They explained that there might be biological differences between men and women in these matters—who could really tell—but if men were as busy as women with professional careers as well as domestic responsibilities, men would not be able to think as clearly and as deeply either. In effect, what the men thought was a biological difference the women preferred to explain as a socially conditioned one.

Virtually all the women said that to survive and to flourish, they had to be strong-willed and single-minded, that they had to work harder than male students. This was necessary because toward the end of their schooling, the men received extra attention. Even those women who became teachers agreed that men were professionally tracked more readily than women. There were no secrets in this matter. We also realized that what is a glass ceiling in the West could be a brick wall in the East. Women teachers rarely ascended to the higher teaching ranks and almost never to high administrative positions.

After graduation, what then? Marriage or career or both? Virtually all interviewees married, often to artists whom they met at school or within the artistic community, and virtually all were divorced a few years later. Most remarried, but a few adamantly remain single. Most had at least one child, a few as single mothers, when they were quite young; and most accepted the fact, albeit with great complaint, that they were the primary caregivers in their families.

Competition between spouses could be keen, even brutal, and in several instances led to divorce. Husbands wanted full-time wives. Wives wanted careers. Husbands were jealous of more-successful wives. Successful wives were, in many instances, willing to sacrifice time and energy, but for some, there were limits. If there were children, the artists' mothers, who had once helped their daughters and who were now grandmothers, acted, when available, as baby-sitters. There was, in effect, a matriarchal system in the raising of children. But a few women acknowledged complicity, in that they did not necessarily trust their husbands with the children or in the kitchen. Since there was no interest in trying to raise the consciousness of men in this regard, they preferred to keep domestic responsibilities for themselves. And then they complained when the men said that they should stay in the kitchen and cook.

The record for getting exhibition space was mixed. Some said that they had no problems, others that they could not network as easily as the men and were therefore handicapped, still others were outraged. A few admitted that because of difficulties in forging a career, they would have preferred to have been born male. But when we prodded them on this issue, things became muddled. They were torn between wanting to be feminine in the sense of being delicate, but at the same time they wanted a career and knew they would have to be aggressive like men. But they did not like being aggressive, since this was not feminine. So perhaps it was better to have been born a man in order to be aggressive. The idea of an aggressive woman was a frightening one and conjured up images of Stalinist bureaucrats. The net result was that they would remain as women, staying more or less passive, and allow themselves to be perpetually hurt and abused by the patriarchical culture.

In their relationships with men, their outlook ranged from accepting ongoing patterns of behavior to believing in their own great strength and in the weakness of men. One women even said that women let men think they run things when in fact women run everything, but this seemed self-delusive. A few were in constant search of a strong man who would take care of them rather than being forced into the role of being the strong mother taking care of their men and their children. Compromises seemed to be out of the question for most. Living alone, although no pleasure, was less difficult for some than becoming involved once again with a weak man. We began to understand that that old line, and book title—"men are from Mars, women are from Venus"—describes life in Russia very well.

When we asked broad, fishing-expedition-type questions concerning differences between paintings by men and women, answers fell into two categories. Either it was impossible to tell because good art is good art regardless of the sex of its maker, or one could tell because women's art looked more sensitive, intuitive, and softer, and less intellectual and rational than men's art. The more successful the woman artist, the less likely she was to see any feminine characteristics in art by women, probably because she wanted her works, in her heart of hearts, to look like a man's. Art by men was clearly the standard. Women's work was inferior. This kind of thinking had as much to do with general stylistic attack (color, brushstroke, composition) as with subject matter. What people referred to as women's art was close to kitsch, which in the United States has no basis in gender, but does so in Russia. Not to be kitschy is to be masculine, according to this formulation. But several artists have begun to understand that painting produced from a woman's point of view does not imply kitsch, but instead can be as tough-minded as any art by a man. So, for example, women are beginning to explore the body, male or female, from their own point of view as well as subject matter that has particular value and resonance for them. Some felt that women are more empathic, more refined, more tender, and more emotional, but this did not imply a greater sentimentality or superficiality. In one or two instances, it meant that women don't paint war scenes. But the paradox here was the contradictory assertion that there might very well be a female vision, but it should be judged with a genderless set of values.

Images of the body raised the most disagreement and concern. For those who did not see the body as another kind of traditional still-life subject, but who thought about it in politicized terms, the body could still be thought about in repressive, prudish, Soviet terms or as an object through which artists could project their own personal concerns and interests. This is not as innocent sounding as it appears to be, in that artists could not readily explore the body for personal reasons until perestroika and the fall of the Soviet government. As a result, painting or sculpting a body, or using one's own body in a performance, initially had and still has as much relevance to feminist or erotic concerns as it does to the still-intoxicating sense of personal freedom to do as one wishes. And here the range is very broad, from images concerned with barbaric medical procedures to sexualized views of nudes as seen from a woman's point of view.

There was general agreement that women are more practical and flexible than men. Probably, this view is more common among those who have artist husbands who refuse to do much else than paint or sculpt. Businesspeople have to be practical. Or to say it another way, several present or former artist husbands did not take part in the day-to-day activities of buying food and paying bills. They do not or cannot compartmentalize as women can. We could not determine if this is endemic in Russian society or something that was picked up in art school, where, we gathered, art is presented almost as a priestly calling rather than as a profession. But because the men do not want to accept daily responsibilities, women said that they are infantile, sap their energies, prevent them from completing tasks, have weaker nervous systems, and lack the spiritual and psychological strength of women. But some women were willing to acknowledge that male identity, compromised by decades of official suppression and the turbulence of the post-Soviet years, may have contributed to the men's weaknesses.

Organizational feminism in the arts is still not very popular, but artists are beginning to realize the necessity for some type of structure to enable them to discover more about their own personal visions as women, to help materially in garnering sales, and to change cultural norms. A combination of information available from the West, still resisted by those who do not want to be overrun, or unmoored, by Western culture, and an improving economic situation should help provoke the desire for change and, with that, a wider exploration of subject matter in the studio and organizational apparatuses outside. The word *feministka* nevertheless still carries negative connotations, and although the climate of opinion is changing, all-women shows are still shunned. But in the past decade, the changes in attitude have been prodigious. The self-imposed internal controls that existed before perestroika and that are still present in many artists, have been lifted. The double life that many led—Soviet on the outside, personal on the inside—has now become a single life for many others. And this is a point that needs to be understood by people in the West. Some of the most perceptive artists said that first they had to discover who they were as people; only then could they figure out who they were as women. The rest will follow in time.

List of Artists, Critics, and Gallery Owners Interviewed

....

Russia

Anna Alchuk
Tania Antoshiina
Tatiana Arzamasova
Gulbakhar Ashimova
Larisa Astrein
Irina Bazileva
Natalia Bragina
Viktoria Buivid
Olga Bulgakova
Natalia Cherkashin
Irina Danilova
Vera Dreznina
Elena Elagina
Marina Elkonina
Tatiana Faidish
Elena Figurina
Zoya Frolova
Rimma Gerlovina
Nonna Goriunova
Ludmila Gorlova
Ekaterina Grigorieva
Elena Gutsenko
Tatiana Hengstler
Natalia Kamenetskaia
Maria Katova
Elena Kedrova
Elena Keller
Vera Khlebnikova
Elena Kitaeva
Elena Korennova

Nina Kotyel
Valentina Kropivnitskaia
Elena Kudinova
Lena Kuprina
Ludmila Kutzenko
Tania Liberman
Elena Malisheva
Daria Machneva
Alena Martinova
Bela Matveeva
Alla Mitrofanova
Irina Mozhaeva
Alena Muntz
Irina Nakhova
Tatiana Nasipova
Tatiana Nazarenko
Natalia Nesterova
Natalia Pershina-
  Yakimanskaia
Elena Preobrazhenskaia
Valentina Pivovarova
Alena Romanova
Aidan Salakhova
Elena Selina
Ani Simonian
Maria Snigirevskaia
Nika Stenberg
Natalia Turnova
Irina Vaninskaia
Nina Volkova
Dasha Zakhunova

Nina Zaretskaia
Natalia Zhilina
Marna Zhukova
Larissa Zvezdochetova

Latvia

Laila Bogustova
Ruta Caupova
Arte Dumpe
Helena Heinrihsone
Ieva Iltnere
Franceska Kirke
Dace Liela
Anita Meldere
Malda Muizule
Liga Purmale
Dzemma Skulme
Anita Zabilevskaia
Lolita Zikmane

Estonia

Concordia Klar
Malle Leis
Silvi Liiva
Regina Lukk
Sirje Runge
Liina Siib
Vive Tolli
Marje Uksine

Notes

· ·

Introduction

1. Renee Baigell and Matthew Baigell, *Soviet Dissident Artists: Interviews after Perestroika* (New Brunswick: Rutgers University Press, 1995).
2. See, for example, Margarita Tupitsyn, "What Happened to the Art of the 'Russian Amazons,'" in Norton Dodge, ed., *Lydia Masterkova: Striving Upward to the Real* (New York: Contemporary Russian Art Center of America, 1983), n.p., Tupitsyn, "Unveiling Feminism: Women's Art in the Soviet Union," *Arts Magazine* 65 (December 1990): 65–66; Ans Gevers, et al., *Maria Serebrjakova, Natalia Turnova, Larissa Rezun-Zvezdotsjotova: A Chicken Is No Bird* (Amsterdam: Picaron Editions/Circ, 1991); Alison Hilton, "Feminism and Gender Values in Soviet Art," in Marianne Lijeström, Erla Mäntysaari, and Arja Rosenholm, eds., *Gender Restructuring in Russian Studies* (Tampere, Finland: University of Tampere, 1993), 103–105; and *Heresies* 7, no. 2 (1992), issue devoted to Russian women artists.
3. A brief list would include Anna Rotkirch and Elina Hoavio-Mannila, eds., *Women's Voices in Russia Today* (Brookfield, Vt.: Dartmouth, 1966); N. Vishneva-Sarafanova, *Soviet Women: A Portrait* (Moscow: Progress, 1981); Tatyana Mamonova, ed., *Women and Russia: Feminist Writings from the Soviet Union* (Boston: Beacon Press, 1984); Mary Buckley, *Women and Ideology in the Soviet Union* (Ann Arbor: University of Michigan Press, 1989); Tatyana Mamonova, *Russian Women's Studies: Essays on Sexism in Soviet Culture* (New York; Pergamon Press, 1989); Francine du Plessix Gray, *Soviet Women: Walking the Tightrope* (New York: Doubleday, 1990); Mary Buckley, *Perestroika and Soviet Women* (New York: Cambridge University Press, 1992); *Peace and Democracy News* 7 (Summer 1993); Nanette Funk and Maga Mueller, eds., *Gender Politics and Post Communist Reflections from Eastern Europe and the Former Soviet Union* (New York: Routledge, 1993); Helena Goscilo, ed., *Fruits of Her Plume: Essays on Contemporary Russian Women's Culture* (Armonk, N.Y.: M. E. Sharpe, 1993); Barbara Evans Clements, *Daughters of Revolution: A History of Women in the U.S.S.R.* (Arlington Heights, Ill.: Harlan Davidson, 1994); Rosalind Marsh, ed. and trans., *Women in Russia*

and Ukraine (New York: Cambridge University Press, 1996); Mary Buckley, *Post-Soviet Women: From the Baltic to Central Asia* (New York: Cambridge University Press, 1996); Helen Goscilo and Beth Holmgren, eds., *Russia Women Culture* (Bloomington: Indiana University Press, 1996); and Valerie Sperling, *Organizing Women in Contemporary Russia: Engendering Transition* (New York: Cambridge University Press, 1999).

4. M. N. Yablonskaya, *Women Artists of Russia's New Age, 1900–1935,* trans. Anthony Patton (New York: Rizzoli, 1990), 10–14.

5. F. I. Rerberg, "On Women's Creativity," manuscript in the Central State Archives of Arts and Literature, fond. 2443 (I) 27: 52–93, cited in Yablonskaya, *Women Artists,* 9.

6. Clements, *Daughters of Revolution,* 18–25.

7. John E. Bowlt, ed. and trans., *Russian Art of the Avant-Garde: Theory and Criticism, 1902–1934* (New York; Thames and Hudson, 1988), 102–110.

8. Clements, *Daughters of Revolution,* 99.

9. Cited in Elizabeth Waters, "Finding a Voice: The Emergence of a Women's Movement," in Funk and Mueller, *Gender Politics,* 288.

10. Carola Hanson and Karin Liden, *Moscow Women: Thirteen Interviews,* trans. Gerry Bothmer, George Blecher, and Lone Blecher (New York: Pantheon Books, 1983), 149.

11. Sperling, *Organizing Women,* 17, 95.

12. Mamonova, *Women and Russia,* xiii.

13. Sperling, *Organizing Women,* 27, 275, 278.

14. Hilton, "Feminism and Gender Values," 104.

15. Ans Gevers, "From Story to Text" in Gevers et al., *Maria Serebrjakova, Natalia Turnova, Larissa Rezun-Zvezdotsjotova,* 22.

BRIEF CHRONOLOGY

1. For more information on these and the immediately following works, see Jo Anna Isaak, "Reflections of Resistance: Women Artists on Both Sides of the *Mir,*" *Heresies* 7, no. 2 (1992): 10; the same essay reprinted in Isaak, *Feminism and Contemporary Art: The Revolutionary Power of Women's Laughter* (New York; Routledge, 1996), 127–132; Margarita Tupitsyn, "U-Turn of the U-topian," in David A. Ross, ed., *Between Spring and Summer: Soviet Conceptual Art in the Era of Late Communism* (Cambridge: MIT Press, 1990), 42–45; and Tupitsyn, *After Perestroika: Kitchenmaids or Stateswomen* (New York: Independent Curators, 1993).

2. For these exhibitions, see Esther Zhezmer, "The First Feminist Art Exhibition in the USSR"; Olesya Turkina and Viktor Mazin, "Dealing with Gender: Two Shows"; and Elena Selina, "Woman Worker," *Heresies* 7, no. 2 (1992): 62–76, 77–79, 80–82; Alla Yefina, "Women and Institutions: The Challenge of Soviet Feminism," *Women Artists News* 15 (Fall 1990): 19; Pauline Michgelsen, "Belles des Arts," in Gevers, *Maria Serebrjakova, Natalia Turnova, Larissa Rezun-Zvezdotsjotova,* 77–79; and Alison Hilton, "Domestic Crafts and Creative Freedom: Russian Women's Art," in Goscilo and Holmgren, *Russia Women Culture,* 370.

3. Natalia Kamenetskaia, "Gender Boundaries," *Women in Art* (Moscow: INO Creative Workshop, 1999), 21.

Mature Artists

1. Svetlana Chernishova, *Vera Dreznina* (Moscow, 1993), 31.
2. See Margarita Tupitsyn, "On Some Sources of Soviet Conceptualism," in Alla Rosenfeld and Norton Dodge, eds., *From Gulag to Glasnost: Nonconformist Art from the Soviet Union* (New York: Thames and Hudson, 1995), 323.
3. Charles Doria, ed., *Russian Samizdat Art* (New York: Willis Locker and Owens, 1986), 78–80; and *Photoglyphs* (New Orleans: New Orleans Museum of Art, 1993), n.p.

The New Generation

1. Anna Alchuk, "The Silent Sex," in Gevers et al., *Maria Serebrjakova, Natalia Turnova, Larissa Rezun-Zvezdotsjotova*, 49.
2. Anna Alchuk, "Gender Aspects in the Works of Moscow Women Artists of the 1980s and 1990s" (in Russian), *Women's Dialogue* 2 no. 18 (1998): 20–22.
3. Kristine Stiles, "Uncorrupted Joy: International Art Actions," in Paul Schimmel, ed., *Out of Actions: Between Performance and the Object, 1949–1979* (New York: Thames and Hudson, 1998), 270.
4. For additional material, see Toby Clark, "The 'New Man's' Body: A Motif in Early Soviet Culture," in Matthew Cullerne Brown and Brandon Taylor, eds., *Art of the Soviets: Painting, Sculpture, and Architecture in a One-Party State, 1917–1992* (Manchester: Manchester University Press, 1993), 33–50.
5. It is reported in Margarita Tupitsyn, "Unveiling Feminism: Women's Art in the Soviet Union," *Arts Magazine* 65 (December 1990): 65–66.
6. *Anita Meldere: To Leave, To Return* (Riga: State Art Museum, 1995), 18.
7. Doloris Cogan, coordinator of Women for Meaningful Summits, located in Elkhart, Indiana, was kind enough to send us the catalogue of an exhibition held in Elkhart in 1993, *Irida in Indiana* (Elkhart, Ind.: Midwest Museum of American Art, 1993), as well as many newspaper clippings from the *Elkhart Truth* and the *South Bend Tribune* that described in glowing terms the exhibition and the coordination between local and Russian officials.
8. Kamenetskaia, "Gender Boundaries," 43.
9. *Happy Childhood* (Moscow: XL Gallery, 1994), n.p.

INDEX

About the Authors

RENEE BAIGELL has taught in the English department and the comparative literature program at Rutgers University. MATTHEW BAIGELL is a professor of art history at Rutgers and has written many books and articles on American art. He is the author of *Jewish American Artists and the Holocaust* (1997) and coeditor of *Artists against War and Fascism: Papers of the First American Artists' Congress* (1986) and *Complex Identities: Jewish Consciousness and Modern Art* (2001) (all with Rutgers University Press). Renee Baigell and Matthew Baigell are coauthors of *Soviet Dissident Artists: Interviews after Perestroika* (Rutgers University Press, 1995).